AN EVER-WIDENING CIRCLE

A Workable Plan
for Women's Bible Studies

by

Naomi Taylor Wright

MULTNOMAH PRESS
Portland, Oregon 97266

Library of Congress Card Catalog Number: 77-18361
ISBN: 0-930014-17-0

To my husband Jim
and our four children
Debbie, Beccy, Jim and Mark

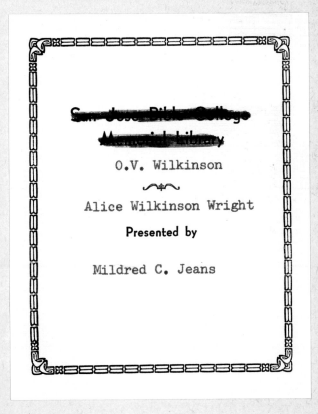

FOREWORD

People are used to seeing church parking lots fill up on Sundays. But when that happens again on Thursday morning – as it does at Bethany Bible Church in Phoenix – people are bound to be curious.

So it was that one day the man whose mortuary is adjacent to the church came over and asked me:

"What goes on in your church Thursday that brings so many cars?"

Happily I told him about the Chris-Town Women's Bible Study, which meets at our church Thursdays. Deciding something lively and exciting was going on, he went home and asked his wife to go to the study!

Not only that full parking lot, but the lives of hundreds of women have been a testimony to our community. At Chris-Town the women are learning how to live the Christian life so that, without saying a word (1 Peter 3:1), they can be effective witnesses for Christ in their homes.

I know many of the people involved in the Chris-Town study. Thus, reading this book was a delight for me as I was able to match names with real people – children of God who are now serving Him in ways which just a few years ago they probably never dreamed possible.

Naomi Wright faithfully recounts the struggles, risks, faith and preparation that went into Chris-Town. She tells about the Chris-Town plan with such splendid detail that many will want to seriously consider if this might also be the route God wants them to use in reaching their own community for Christ.

Chris-Town is not just a women's Bible study, although the cars which fill our lot each Sunday are driven there by women. Through couples' potlucks and evening Bible studies it's also reaching the men – husbands who thirsted for more of God's Word, as well as those who were baffled and enchanted, and often later drawn to the Lord through the silent testimony of wives living for Jesus Christ.

-Dr. John L. Mitchell, Senior Pastor
Bethany Bible Church
Phoenix, Arizona

ABOUT THE AUTHOR

Women who sit under the teaching ministry of Naomi Wright say she has "a way of bringing the Bible right down to where we live." Hundreds in the Phoenix area come to the Chris-Town Women's Bible Study, which she teaches.

Naomi's preparation as an effective Bible teacher began in Salt Lake City, where as a 17-year-old she accepted Christ as her Savior in a Youth for Christ meeting. For the next two years she attended an evening Bible study. But her eagerness to learn more of God's Word led her to enroll at Multnomah School of the Bible in Portland, Ore., where she also worked with the Young Life program. While at Multnomah she met Jim, and they where married in 1950.

In addition to raising a family of four (she is also twice a grandmother), Naomi taught Sunday school, teen Bible studies and children's classes. For four summers the family ministered together at Trout Creek Bible camp near Portland – Jim as program director, the children on work crew and Naomi teaching teen girls and women staff members.

The Chris-Town study, which she and her next-door friend started in 1959 with a handful of neighbors, grew to 650, divided, and again had grown to 650 by the fall of 1977.

Jim and Naomi are members of Bethany Bible Church in Phoenix. Jim, now an assistant principal at Washington High School in Phoenix, has taught adult Sunday school and church membership classes for many years. He also played an important role in developing Chris-Town's couples' potlucks and evening Bible studies.

Despite the load of teaching and counseling the Chris-Town study means for Naomi, she guards her time to make sure her family comes first. She keeps her speaking engagements to a minimum, and these primarily around Phoenix.

The success and ministry of Chris-Town have brought many requests for help in beginning similar Bible studies elsewhere. A few she has been able to assist personally, but the demand became so great that she was urged to write this book about the Chris-Town method.

ACKNOWLEDGMENTS

As with any work of God, this book has been a cooperative venture.

From the beginning it was recognized that some would write, some type, some do the correcting – but God would put it all together.

Contained throughout the whole book are experiences from real lives and I wish to thank each one for allowing me to share them with you.

My sincere thanks go first to all those who were my faithful teachers that I, in turn, might teach others.

I also want to express my appreciation to all those who with their love and hard work have made the Bible study possible these 18 years. If it were not for them there would have been no Chris-Town and thus, no book.

Special thanks go to:

Dr. John L. Mitchell, pastor of Bethany Bible Church in Phoenix, and the church staff and board, for the use of their facilities which enabled Chris-Town to grow.

Cherie Williams, for writing Chapter 6.

Phyllis Lyon, Carlotta Ott, Evelyn Boyce, Peggy Hochstetler and others who read a part or the whole of the manuscript and made suggestions and additions.

Peggy Gustave and Erma Hardin for typing most of the first manuscript.

Jeanne Doering of Multnomah Press, for her invaluable assistance in editing the book.

Most of all, to my beloved husband Jim, for his tender love and encouragement throughout these years of Bible study and the writing of this book. He has made many wise suggestions and corrections and wiped away a few tears from my eyes when things got rough.

But above all, to our wonderful Lord . . . for this has been His doing and we all rejoice together and are glad.

Naomi Taylor Wright
Phoenix, Arizona

CONTENTS

BEGINNINGS

Drop a pebble into a pond and you'll see ever-widening circles spread out over the surface of the water. Eighteen years ago a pebble dropped in my home started a circle of Christ's love which has flowed out of my kitchen, out of my city of Phoenix, and even out of Arizona and across the sea.

The pebble was a question by my neighbor and friend, Jackie. One day she walked into my kitchen and asked, "Naomi, what is sin?" From that question grew a circle which has now encompassed thousands of women, who are experiencing the reality of Jesus in their homes.

For years I had been praying for a neighborhood Bible study. But that day, there in my own kitchen, in my own world, when Jackie's question about sin opened that opportunity, I was embarrassed, surprised and flustered.

I wasn't expecting God to answer like this. There was another neighbor who had said to me, "Naomi, I have decided that I do not want to receive the Lord. I am not interested in becoming a Christian." I was bewildered by her response. Now, I wondered, would Jackie recoil the same way if I tried to answer her questions about sin and the work of Jesus Christ? I surely didn't want to lose the confidence of my next-door friend.

Groping for words, I tried to tell Jackie of God's love for her and of His hate for sin. As Jackie hungrily and honestly asked one question after another, I began to relax, realizing this was an opportunity planned by God. He was right there in the kitchen as we talked!

BIRTH OF A STUDY

Jackie wanted to know more. Our children played together as we mothers talked out Jackie's questions – outside hanging up the wash, inside sprucing up the kitchen, attacking my self-perpetrating ironing basket or sometimes simply sitting down together with our Bibles.

But a good thing got to be too much – and the time I was spending with Jackie started to tell on my four young children. To become more efficient in our homes and study time, we cut our time together to one hour a day. For that hour Jackie and I would discuss the good things she had learned, and she asked the questions she encountered during her study of the Bible since the previous day.

For the next six months, Jackie (who had received the Lord as her Savior when she was a child) grew like a spiritual sunflower, reaching up and out to God. For years she had eagerly searched for a knowledge of God. Through our study of God's Word she came to this knowledge. Our hearts rejoiced as both of our prayers were being answered.

Then came the day when she posed a question which shocked me almost as much as her first question about sin.

"Naomi," she said, "this is too good to keep to ourselves. Why don't we invite the neighbors?"

That old fear of rejection surged through me again. "They won't come," I replied, vividly recalling that experience with my other neighbor.

Jackie offered a solution. "Oh, I'll go ask them – if you'll teach."

She was persuasive. As she started to figure out the specifics – who to contact, when to have the meeting, what to do with the children – I thought of how much I had prayed about a Bible study for my neighborhood. For years it seemed that God's answer was "wait." Now He was flashing a vivid, verdant "go" and apparently wanted me to teach it!

GOD'S PLANNING

I began to see how He had prepared me for this role. An ever-widening circle of God's love had begun in my own life at the age of 17, when I accepted the Lord as my Saviour at a Youth for Christ meeting in Salt Lake City, Utah. I was encouraged to get into a Bible study. I did – and this study became so important to me that I'd turn down dates if they interfered with this "date" with God. Some day, I thought, I might be privileged to be the one who teaches.

Now, this "some day" had come.

Jackie was busy figuring arrangements.

"We could turn my third bedroom into a nursery," she said. "Matthew won't mind sharing his toys. I'll ask my husband but I'm sure it will be okay."

"How about babysitters?" I ventured. "We can't use high school girls because they will be in school."

"We'll find someone," Jackie responded. And we did. One woman was hired to watch the babies. Ruby, one of our church members, would tell Bible stories and teach songs to the preschoolers. We paid the sitters from what the women placed in a bowl on the table we had labeled, "$10 needed for sitters." As the Bible study continued, Jackie often personally made up the difference if enough was not given.

My kitchen quickly filled with neighbors that first day of our study. Sitting together around the table, we started a verse-by-verse study of the Gospel of John. From week to week the women returned, commenting about how they enjoyed studying and sharing what they had learned. Then the unexpected happened. Two were offended by a statement about a certain doctrine and, despite our attempt to handle the situation tactfully, refused to return. We were very disappointed, but as we continued our study in John, we saw that people even turned from Jesus when He faced them with hard decisions.

A COMFORTABLE NINE

Seven neighbors came as "regulars" and with Jackie and me that made nine – a comfortable group to encircle my kitchen table. Then some of the women asked if they could invite their mothers, sisters or friends. We wondered before saying yes whether we could handle a larger group and the extra children more women would bring.

I shared the dilemma with my husband, Jim, who had prayed with me from the beginning about starting a Bible study.

"I'm not sure it would be wise to let it grow," Jim cautioned, "if a larger group would mean more work and more telephoning. Remember you also have a high school Sunday school class. I don't want you to harm your health or our home."

I knew Jim was right. To serve the Lord best, I needed to put my family first. As we talked we came up with a plan. If Jackie could coordinate all the details, enlisting women to help her, that would free me to concentrate on the teaching. And that way, I could handle a larger group. We also decided on some rules for telephoning connected to the study. No one was to call me in the evening except for an emergency. Evenings were strictly for my family.

We also decided to seek advice from someone who had led a larger Bible study. Jackie and I drove across town to where Orean Howard (Mrs. Grant Howard Sr.) led 50 women in a Bible study at the spacious home of

Christian friends. For 15 years Orean had also conducted a Bible study in Tucson, Arizona, which continues under another teacher.

Her advice encouraged us. "Trust in the Lord, girls," she said. "If God sends you more women to love and to teach, He will provide all your needs as they come up. She pointed us to two verses in Philippians, 4:13 and 4:19: "I can do all things through Christ which strengtheneth me," and, "But my God shall supply all your need according to his riches in glory by Christ Jesus." These were just the right passages for our doubts and fears.

Orean also suggested that I teach separate books of the Bible rather than topically. "That way you teach the whole Word of God and not just favorite passages and subjects," she said. We had started right by studying the Gospel of John.

MORE BABYSITTERS

Believing God would have us grow we prayed for more babysitters. Young mothers who came wanted to get in on the Bible study and have a break from their children. God answered that prayer when several women were hired through a nearby church. Spare cribs and playpens came out of attics and garages.

We reminded the women that they would have to help if the study group were to grow. They agreed to handle the various tasks. The okay to invite others worked like fertilizer on an anemic lawn. The next Thursday it seemed everyone was swarming to my house. One friend filled her car to bulging with young mothers and children. Another brought her sister-in-law and someone else came with her mother and two sisters, who were visiting from out-of-town. Obviously, we couldn't all fit in the kitchen, so we borrowed tables and placed them in a U-shape in the living room.

Growth brought other problems which were tests for me. I'm the "sit-down" type leader. I'd rather not stand in front of people. As long as the groups remained small, I could sit at the tables with the rest of the women and lead the discussion. One day that had to come to an end.

"Naomi, we just can't hear you," the women complained. "Can you stand up?"

I balked. But there was no other solution. Reluctantly I gave up my chair.

This battle over sitting or standing was to be the first of several things God put before me as the group grew. Each time, like Moses (Exodus 4:10-14) I argued with God that I couldn't do it. But He won. And now I am thankful that He did, and that He didn't have to send someone else to do the job that He wanted me to do — as He had to send an Aaron to speak for Moses.

COUNSELING CHALLENGES

The increasing need for counseling was another area where I had to obey God. I didn't feel I knew how to help the women with their problems, but God showed me that they desperately needed a listening, caring heart — someone detached from their situation. And — God had promised in James 1:5 to supply the necessary wisdom.

I remember one late-night phone call from the husband of one young woman in the study group. She wanted a divorce and had locked him out of the house. Rather than telling the husband how wrong the wife was, I sought to find out what he might be doing to contribute to the problem.

"Will you go see her, please?" he pleaded.

"Did she ask me to come?" I asked, remembering that we should not try to counsel a person who does not ask for help.

"No," he replied. "But she likes you and I think she will talk to you."

I told him I would go to see her on one condition: that he would allow me to call him back and tell him some of the things that were bothering her, and that we would talk them over.

"Sure, anything," he said gratefully.

Reluctantly his wife let me in. She said she'd already made up her mind. But as we talked over a cup of coffee she began to weep and I saw that she still loved her husband. I believed there was hope. We sat and talked of God's plan for our lives and His love for our homes and marriages. She opened up and shared her problems with me.

Two hours later I called the husband back and told him three things that most bothered his wife. He was very willing to listen and to admit that he was wrong. We talked about why he had been wrong and came up with some suggestions for a change of direction. Later he called his wife, apologized, and told her how he planned to change some things. And they were reunited.

Through this God taught me to counsel *the one who calls*, because that partner is the one interested in saving the marriage.

A WELCOME DAY OUT

Love between the Bible study women and me grew and we began to really look forward to each Thursday. For all of us it was a welcome day "out" with our friends, and the time was invested rather than wasted. Those of us with little children no longer felt imprisoned by the walls of our homes. Some noticed they were less demanding of their husband's attention because they could relate to friends with similar needs. We were sisters in Christ, no matter what our age or status in life.

Then we decided to have simple luncheons each Thursday. Along with their Bibles and notebooks, the women brought heads of lettuce, stalks of celery and cans of tuna fish. Together we fixed a salad, warmed up garlic bread and with iced tea prepared for a feast after our study. Mothers with very little ones fed them while the others prepared the luncheon. The older children brought little sack lunches for a picnic out under the trees with their sitters.

Husbands noticed changes in their wives. The women would come home from the Thursday studies with new enthusiasm and purpose. And they worked harder during the week so they could take Thursdays off for their time with the "gals."

After a year and a half, our group had grown from just two (Jackie and me) to 39. Then another problem emerged. Some of those coming to the Bible study had never studied Scripture before. Some had studied the Bible for years. Could we meet these diverse needs with only one class? Someone suggested holding two classes a week — one for the women who knew little about the Bible or had just become Christians, and another for the more mature Christians.

I saw immediately that the proposal wouldn't work.

"If I taught two days a week, I would have less time for my family," I explained. "Besides, this would keep a woman from bringing a visitor who didn't fit into the same level group."

Another suggestion — having second-hour study groups geared to various needs — seemed more reasonable. But before we could try a second-hour system, Jackie moved away. Her departure left a big void in our group leadership and in our nursery situation.

GOD HAD SOLUTIONS

But God was already preparing solutions to both of these problems. Another woman stepped in as coordinator and a friend offered use of her large home, which was located near a good Bible-teaching church which allowed us to use its nursery facilities.

A few weeks later, settled into our new location, we decided to start the second-hour groups. The first hour we met together to study a book of the Bible, verse-by-verse, relating it to our personal lives and family relationships. The second hour we broke into smaller groups led by Christian women who were part of the larger group. Women who were just looking into Christianity gathered out on the patio in the warm Arizona sunshine for a basic Bible study we called "Getting to Know Jesus." Another group met in the family room and studied "The Walk of Fellowship of the Believers." A third group, called "Digging Deeper," met in the living room to study a book of the Bible.

Over the spring and summer our group almost doubled in size to 69. We had just about outgrown our second home. As the Bible study went into its third year we knew another move was ahead. My sister-in-law suggested we check into the Chris-Town Auditorium, located in a shopping mall in our community and about half a mile from the same church. Officials told us we could have free use of the large auditorium and its kitchen! (Why is it that we pray about some need and then are surprised when God answers beautifully? That never ceases to amaze me!) Now we could continue having the studies — and the potluck luncheons which now were monthly instead of weekly.

We always believed it was important to make visitors feel important, because most had never been to a Bible study before and were apprehensive. Many said that fear made the climb up the stairwell to the Chris-Town Auditorium the longest they ever took. Some actually expected to walk into a room full of grim-faced elderly women, shuffling around in homely dresses and their hair severely combed back into tight buns. (Christians, you know, have quite a reputation!) Instead they found very ordinary women, young and older, just like themselves, wearing bright, stylish clothes. They were greeted with smiles, a name tag and coffee or iced tea.

MORE GROWTH PAINS

Our welcome to visitors caused them to want to come again and bring their friends. So growth pains set in again and I was soon faced with another challenge from God. The women thought I should use a microphone!

Now, some people find using mikes as natural as licking a lollipop. But I had some real fears of the contraption. And then when tape recorders started to appear on the tables — and I realized people would be listening to me over and over, mistakes and all — this added yet another fear.

As I prayed for courage God brought the right Scriptures to my situation. When I was afraid of faces, He showed me Jeremiah 1:8: "Be not afraid of their faces: for I am with thee to deliver thee, saith the Lord." When I was discouraged, He sent me to Deuteronomy 1:21: "Behold, the Lord thy God hath set the land before thee: go up and possess it, as the

Lord God of thy fathers hath said to thee; fear not, neither be discouraged." He had shown me, as He showed Moses, that He would be with my mouth and teach it what to say (Exodus 4:12).

"Oh Lord, I do trust you," I now prayed. "Your promise in Isaiah 26:3 is for me 'Thou wilt keep him (me!) in perfect peace whose mind is stayed on Thee for he (I!) trusteth in Thee.' "

He kept His promise of peace and I was ready to meet any microphones and tape recorders they'd come up with!

The Chris-Town Auditorium was our Bible study home for five and a half years. From it we took our name: The Chris-Town Women's Bible Study. When our average attendance reached 150 we outnumbered the chairs and some women were sitting on tables for the lecture hours. The small groups were crowded around tables and it was hard to hear because most groups met in the same room. The situation was not good. One teacher took her second-hour group to a room in a nearby bank to alleviate the noise and congestion. But that didn't help the problems of first-hour attendance. We didn't want to split the group. Obviously we had to think about moving again.

Our next move was to a large cafeteria. But our time schedule conflicted with theirs and after a few months we knew it wouldn't work out. There seemed to be no other place in all of Phoenix. Every possibility charged $50 and up for each weekly meeting. And these places had no nursery or small rooms for our group studies.

EXTREMITIES ARE OPPORTUNITIES

At that point we learned, as someone once said, that our extremities are God's opportunities. The problems forced us to look to church facilities although, short of borrowing nursery space, we had avoided meeting in a church. To do so, we felt, might keep some women from coming either because it wasn't their church or they simply felt uncomfortable inside church walls.

After praying about it, we believed God would take care of this problem, too. We decided to contact a good Bible-believing church. Our letter went to Bethany Bible Church, which had opened its nursery facilities to us for six years. When the church board voted to allow us to use all available rooms for only $10 a week, we felt that God had confirmed His choice to us. Church staff members were especially cooperative as we made the transition, and the church's large parking lot accommodated our ever-increasing number of cars.

We wondered at first if some women would quit coming because we'd moved to a church. Instead, they kept coming and brought their friends. Many commented on the loving attitude they found at the study. Every week we heard comments such as, "I never felt so loved as here," "Everyone really cares about each other," and, "I wish I would have come when my friend first invited me several years ago." As we heard these that you are My disciples, if you have love for one another" (John 13:35 NASB).

The good things happening in our women's Bible study reached the ear of the religious editor of the *Phoenix Republic*, who then prepared a full-page Sunday section story with pictures on several of the Phoenix Bible studies. It was hard for her to believe that so many people could get together and study the Bible without disputing over church differences. The interview enabled us to share how we were talking about the One who unifies us, rather than about things that might divide us. "Christianity is a relationship, not a religion," I told the editor. "There are times we disagree, but we try to disagree agreeably. We have had few major disagreements throughout all these years. God has given us grace to deal with these problems as they have come up and the minor issues are taken care of as we get into Scripture. When we believe what the Bible says we find that there are not so many places that we differ, after all."

OUTREACH WIDENS

The ever-widening circle of God's love through the women began to draw others to our study. Women began coming from many of the surrounding areas — Scottsdale, Tempe, Mesa, Chandler, Glendale, Litchfield Park, Laveen, Paradise Valley and Black Canyon City. One woman and several of her friends drove two hours, one way, each week from Payson. Another came with her tiny baby two hours from Globe, seeking help.

Many of the women coming to the Bible study were seeking help for special personal needs. Many could not afford professional counseling for their troubled marriages. Some were already looking into divorce. As they found out that God loved them and had a plan for their lives, many accepted Christ as Saviour and Lord. As new Christians or renewed Christians they began to let the Holy Spirit have control of their lives. They reached out in love to their husbands, and the husbands responded to the "new" wives and in time became the lovers and leaders God intended them to be.

As the wives changed, we found husbands began asking if there was some place that they could go to hear some of the same things that were bringing such joy and purpose into the lives of their wives. Our solution was couples' evening potlucks. The women would ask their husbands for a "date" to a delicious feast (and what man doesn't like to eat?). This would include get-acquainted times, special music and a testimony by one of the men who had become a Christian, often as a result of the change he saw in his wife. The men would then be invited to a couples' evening Bible study.

The evening Bible studies became a special place where the husband and wife could together learn about the Lord. The men were put under no pressure either to speak or to pray. Often they would fearfully come "just once," but come back again and again. In the end, many became involved in Bible-teaching churches and developed into Christian leaders.

800 AND BULGING

In the fifteenth year of our Thursday morning Bible study we had grown unbelievably. Some 800 women were on the rolls and 650 attended regularly. Two church nurseries cared for 350 children five years of age and under. The church which had been our study home for the past eight years was bulging. Some mothers had to hold their children on their laps, while others sat on the floor in the foyer at our peak time. We needed two guest groups, and we needed to expand our selection of second-hour classes. But we were absolutely out of room.

When we prayed about what to do, the answer became very obvious. It was time to multiply by dividing. God had prepared the way for this decision. A pastor in another area of town had been praying that a women's Bible study start in his church. His church was located near where 150 of our women already lived, and in the area where we wanted to start another study. The Lord led one woman to be the teacher and 14 others to be group leaders.

Seeing now how God has touched the lives of hundreds and even thousands of women through the Chris-Town Bible study, it is hard to believe that at one time the study was only the prayer of two women, one who had the desire to teach and one who had the desire to learn.

He opened the way for us to share Christ with our neighbors and friends. He provided places where we could meet. He arranged care facilities for the children. He prompted us to begin small groups for individualized study. He made our home life more beautiful as we learned together how to be better wives and mothers.

You may already have a successful Bible study, and, if so, we join in gratefulness to God for what He is doing through you. You may, on the other hand, want to modify your study by some of the things that worked for Chris-Town, or even start a study of your own.

This book will tell how to go about starting a large or small Bible study. It will also share insights for counseling, improving husband-wife relationships, winning husbands to the Lord, and growing as couples into mature, godly, happy people who love and serve God together.

THE IMPERATIVE

Radio announcer Larry Wright was on his way to the top. People all over Phoenix knew the voice of "Lucky Lawrence." But as success poured in at the studio, his life crumbled at home. He and his wife Sue considered divorce.

"Ours was the typical, sad story of success," Larry says. "We filled our lives with things and then found these did not bring happiness. It was the same old plot — a husband who turns to alcohol and a wife who tries to arrange a life of her own."

Sue's search for peace of mind brought her to faith in Jesus Christ through a Bible-teaching church. She began attending regularly the Chris-Town Bible study.

"In a matter of months I began to see Jesus come alive in my wife," Larry said. "I couldn't deny the reality of it. I watched as she learned what God wanted her to be, and how she depended on Him to bring it about. And my life was touched. I, too, wanted to commit my life to Jesus Christ."

In the meantime, the women of Chris-Town study were praying about ways to reach their unsaved husbands with the Gospel and to involve them in other Bible studies. They planned a special evening study, just for couples. Larry came to the first — and through that study came to know the Lord.

"Without the Chris-Town Women's Bible Study," Larry said, "I am convinced that Sue and I would be divorced today and I am equally sure that I would not know Jesus Christ as my Savior and Lord."

The story of Chris-Town Bible Study is replete with experiences similar to Larry's and Sue's — couples who become one in Christ because the husband was drawn to the Lord through the transformed life of his wife.

A SOURCE OF PEACE AND HOPE

The story of Chris-Town is also one of women who seek peace — and find the One who gives peace. It is women who have lost hope — and find the One who gives hope.

Phoenix doesn't have a monopoly on people with problems. When Ann, one of our group leaders, moved to California, she immediately sought a women's Bible study to attend. To her amazement, the leaders of the large group she attended declared it "full" and turned away many women. Ann's heart ached for these women. She began to pray about beginning another study and talked with her pastor about possibly starting a study in the church. He was delighted with the idea. As the study was started, Ann was able to use many of the skills she had learned during the years she was a group leader at Chris-Town.

Because the church was located near a Marine base, the Bible study had an outreach to many servicemen's wives. In time some of the men were transferred, and three of the wives were able to begin new studies in their new locations.

When Ann and her husband recently moved back to Phoenix, she was thrilled to see that the group she started was able to carry on and continue a vital ministry among military wives.

My Aunt Dorothy in Wyoming is working with young married women, and also sees a great need to reach women for Christ. She writes, "If I can help just one woman find real happiness, I will be happy, too. There are so many unhappy homes today."

The despair and turmoil in lives today is astonishing. Evangelist Billy Graham says he gets from 5,000 to 10,000 letters a day, most of them from people who say they are lonely, empty, have domestic problems or other cares. Most are ultimately asking, "Is there any hope for me?"

AGELESS SITUATIONS

The situation wasn't much different about 2,000 years ago:

> *And seeing the multitudes, He felt compassion for them, because they were distressed and downcast like sheep without a shepherd.* (Matthew 9:36 NASB)

Part of the problem today may be that we are unaware of the problems people have. They may appear happy on the outside, all smiles, a firm handshake, laughter. So we are surprised when they commit suicide — or disappear from home, tearfully trace the development of a divorce, or are arrested for beating their children.

I remember two women who attended a Christian women's luncheon a few years ago. They looked like they had stopped at the boutique and beauty solon just before coming. They were elegant — not a hair out of place. They sat and looked like queens with every part of their empire under control. If anyone had asked me to pick out the people in that group with problems, those ladies would have been last on my list. Yet after I spoke they were among the first to come seeking counsel for personal problems.

You can't tell by looks who needs Christ. All do — the affluent, the poor, the good, the bad, the disinterested and the interested. Jesus told His disciples:

> *The harvest is plentiful, but the workers are few. Therefore beseech the Lord of the harvest to send out workers into His harvest. (Matthew 9:37-38 NASB)*

We can't limit God. That's what I tried to do when Jackie first suggested starting a Bible study. I thought none of the neighbors would be interested. So I was reluctant to invite them. But Jackie did. And they came.

PEOPLE ARE INTERESTED

Probably one of the biggest drawbacks to sharing Christ is our faulty assumption that people are not interested. They *are* interested. They have deep human needs and want something to fill that need. For nearly two decades women have been coming to Chris-Town because:

1. They find that needed "something" is a *Someone*, Jesus Christ;

2. They find that God has a plan for their lives which includes filling those needs;

3. They discover it is possible for them to become the women God meant for them to be, by applying His Word to their daily lives;

4. They find that they never stop learning from God's Word; and even those who have known the Lord for some time can learn while they are serving in teaching and helping others.

The heart of Chris-Town Bible Study is Titus 2:4-5. Here God charges older women with a special responsibility to:

> ... *teach the young women to be sober, to love [Greek = to show affection to] their husbands, to love their children, to be*

discreet, chaste, keepers at home, good, obedient to their own husbands, that the Word of God be not blasphemed.

God has strengthened our Bible study through mature older women. They come to our group feeling there is no place for them to serve. But at Chris-Town they find there is a special place for them: to love, serve and encourage other women. The ministry pattern of older women teaching younger women is not without a reverse effect, however. Many of our older women find true satisfaction in that their needs were met as they worked with younger women.

THE OLDER WOMEN

Ruth speaks to that experience: "It was the three youngest members of the group who really took me in that first morning I was in your class. Karen said I reminded her of her grandmother. That did it — we were friends! As you spoke that day on Proverbs 31 I sat amazed. All this in that precious little book! And I had missed it? One verse hit me right between the eyes: 'She openeth her mouth with wisdom; and in her tongue is the law of kindness' (Proverbs 31:26). I soon found myself more earnestly seeking the guidance of the Holy Spirit. I wanted the words from my mouth, especially as related to family life, to be His words, and reflect His manner. The result even surprised me! One night my husband said, 'Here comes my sweetheart!' Now, my husband is the quiet, unexpressive type, so that was really something for which to praise the Lord!"

Leah is another of the special older women. The first day she came, 2½ years after the Bible study began, she felt God's tug on her heart to stay and help us. Many of the women regard her as their favorite group leader. She could easily teach the first-hour Bible study, but she lovingly supports and prays for me and has often taught the lesson when I have not been able to teach. A woman of great wisdom, she counsels many of the women and has helped me when I have had teenager problems in my own home.

Louise is another older colleague. She already had a ministry with young girls but her heart was so full that she wanted to help us reach our Bible study women. That was a year and a half after the study started and we began having a "guest group" to which the usually-apprehensive first-timers would be taken after the first-hour lecture. In her loving way Louise presents the Gospel and then allows the women to make up their own minds. She does not push them nor put them on the spot, believing that the Holy Spirit is the only One who can bring about the new birth, anyway. She is available to pray with them if they wish, or to counsel on a problem they might have.

But the leadership we have enjoyed through older women does not mean that younger women cannot teach. If the younger woman is growing, loving and Spirit-filled, she may have a place of leadership, realizing there will be limitations to her counseling. Barb, who moved to Hawaii, was sought out by an older woman for counsel, and was able to help her in the areas where she had learned to be a godly, loving, responsive wife.

AN AID TO PASTORS

Pastors do not have the time to counsel all the women in their churches. And frequently, although well-trained, they are unable to speak to a woman's deepest needs. Thus God has directed the older women to carry this special responsibility, not to usurp the authority of pastors but to aid them.

Many pastors counsel couples before marriage, but in truth counseling needs continue after marriage. We find that Bible study helps meet their needs. Many couples will not go to a counselor until the problem is almost beyond help. But we thank God for the hundreds of homes which have been changed through women's Bible studies as women learned from other women who were spiritually-sensitive, and became the wives God intended them to be.

Some may suggest that annual or semi-annual women's retreats could take care of this need. But conferences and retreats, worthy as they are, tend to overwhelm women with too much information. They best learn — and change — slowly.

Their needs are diverse. When we asked women, "What is the greatest desire of your heart?", we received answers like these:

- To know what God really wants me to do, and then for Him to guide me to accomplish it.
- To be a spirit-filled Christian, walking daily in His will, living in His praise.
- To be closer to God and to have a Christian home.
- To win my husband for the Lord.
- To put God into my everyday life.
- To be a real living testimony for the Lord.
- To know the Bible more completely so that I can freely counsel and help people according to His Word.
- To learn to handle problems at home without severe anxiety.
- To learn how to have devotions and be consistent in them.
- To be able to tell the unsaved about God's great love, and to feed new Christians.

WHERE NEEDS ARE MET

Women will go where their needs are being met. They'll come to Bible study if it meets their needs. Often a woman may be struggling with some aspect of forgiveness or a poor self-concept. This was the case of one young wife who wrote: "The first time I ever attended the Bible study I felt a real love and friendship from, and around, everyone. I guess I love Bible study most because I am learning how to serve the Lord. I never knew how to turn my problems over to Him, but the Bible study teaches me how. I never liked myself very much before but I find that as I turn these things over to the Lord and He changes me into the woman He wants me to be, that I am not so bad after all. The Bible study also teaches me how to love my husband as he wants to be loved. And he really likes that, too!"

Libraries, bookstores and community service programs offer books and schools for women on how to sew, cook, repair and look pretty. But none of these reach to a woman's deepest needs and the yearnings of her soul. Women's Bible studies are not an incidental. They are a necessity for effectively communicating from one generation to another the instructions God has given for ways to live pleasing Him. And they are one of His most effective tools of evangelism.

Some in the evangelical world have voiced objections to women's Bible studies. They point to the dangers of groups functioning outside the church — dangers of wrong doctrine, wrong emphases and other damaging results. Often as these influential and respected Christians give these opinions in churches across the country, they unknowingly address men and women who are in those pews only because Jesus Christ became real to them through a women's or couples' Bible study. Sometimes these very ones who speak out against Bible studies were themselves won to the Lord through a home Bible study and there got their first spiritual training.

ANSWERING OBJECTIONS

I would like to answer some of the most common objections:

Objection #1: "The studies take women (and their husbands, if they attend couples' studies) away from the church."

Answer: I remember that even my own church looked dubiously at the Bible study when we first began. Not so now. Helen Zahn, a charter member of the church, recently wrote to me: "Any misgivings or apprehensions about the class and the relationship or effect of it on the church have long since been laid to rest. It's been positive all the way."

Her husband Don, also a charter member who served on the church board many, many years, commented: "I have observed that the women's Bible study class has been a unique and effective evangelistic outreach in our community. The ministry, although unofficial in Bethany Bible Church, has received the whole-hearted support of the church officials."

Don further remarked: "The evidence is clear that the class has been a great source of encouragement in Christian growth through the study of the Word of God as it applies to day-by-day living. Many young women have been led to a saving knowledge of Jesus Christ, bringing their husbands and families into this knowledge, too. Our church and other churches have had the privilege of seeing many of these families become a part of the fellowship of the church. Without formal publicity or fanfare, the teaching, prayer, personal counseling and Christian fellowship have produced mature Christians. I am confident that a spiritual heritage is being built from week to week through these classes."

There are actually several wrinkles to the objection that Bible studies take people away from church. One is that women become so involved in a Bible study that they become too busy to be active in church. But at Chris-Town we encourage the women to have one responsibility at church and one at Bible study. We discourage them from getting too busy outside of their homes. We all have heard of homes that have suffered deeply, or that have broken up, because somebody became a "churchaholic" or "seminar-aholic" or "Bible-studiaholic" and neglected the home.

Another part of this objection is that a Bible study robs a church of its members — either because they make the Bible study a substitute for church or leave the first church for a second.

Instead, we have found that churches are welcoming whole families which never attended before. I remember one woman who received Christ through our Bible study. The following six weeks, she, her husband and children attended church. The difference in their lives astonished and intrigued a friend who asked if she could go with them!

In many cases the husband is unsaved and does not want to go to church. If he permits the wife to attend, we encourage her to go without him. However, we warn her not to run out of the house every time the church doors are open, leaving her husband alone, or, worse yet, causing him to seek companionship elsewhere — because his wife is not home. If she lovingly submits herself to her husband, he will come, in time. We have seen it happen many times.

The opposite is also true. If she goes ahead to church against his spoken or unspoken desire, he will begin to call her a fanatic. This will hinder his coming to Christ — or taking the lead if he is a Christian — and this often ends in a standoff with the wife saying, "I am to put the Lord first and, therefore, if my husband doesn't like it, it is his problem that we are unhappy." We teach women that it is not a wife's job to be her husband's Holy Spirit. She is to love him and leave the results to God. She is to obey God by obeying her husband. We have witnessed overwhelming results to this truth. An obedient woman may, in time, have the joy of sitting with her whole family in church.

We compete with no church. We believe we are an arm of the church because, in teaching women to love God and their families and to become godly women, we are helping the church strengthen its testimony. God said that if the home is not right, the "Word of God will be blasphemed" (Titus 2:5). The local church is only as strong as its homes.

We encourage women to pray about finding a strong Bible-teaching church if they are not already in one. Therefore, hunger for the Word and for better teaching does prompt some families to leave modernistic churches for churches which emphasize a personal relationship with Christ and regular Bible study.

Several years ago Wilma came to our Bible study because a broken arm prevented her from working for a while. She had been a minister's daughter and raised in a religious home. She always assumed that she was a "Christian." But she wasn't prepared for the Christianity she encountered at the Bible study.

"I was shocked on my first day at the study," she recalls. "It really disturbed me to see women scribbling on the pages of their Bibles. My Bible was neat and clean — but it was also somewhere at home and probably dusty. My attendance at church and support of church organizations and activities gave me a sense of doing what was pleasing to God. I was proud of my denomination but ignorant of spiritual truths. At the age of 57, I went through much turmoil and arguing with God before I could admit aloud that being born in a parsonage might be a social asset, but it wouldn't get me into heaven. When I surrendered my stubborn pride and accepted Christ, I was filled with a great peace and my inner joy was shared by my Christian friends. I learned later in Luke 15:10 that even the angels rejoiced when this grandma yielded herself to Jesus Christ."

It wasn't long before Wilma, her husband Bob and another couple from their church began coming to an evening Bible study. Their spiritual lives were growing rapidly as they studied the Word of God in a group. Later her husband led a Bible study in their home for a year. They got into a good Bible church and later, at retirement, became missionary houseparents for Wycliffe Bible Translators.

Objection #2: "Without church supervision, there is a possibility of teaching error."

Answer: Error is a possibility in any area of God's work. In church and out, many errors are being taught as "truth" in the name of the Lord. There is no way anyone can police every pastor or teacher. In our women's Bible study we try to stay in the Word, relying on the Holy Spirit to teach us. All our leaders are maturing in their Christian walk. We insist that each group leader be in harmony with our doctrinal positions and that each fill out a four-page doctrinal questionnaire before she is even trained for leadership. If someone departs from the doctrinal positions to an important degree, we tell her that for her sake and ours it would be best if she not teach.

The content of my teaching is checked several ways. I can talk with my husband Jim, who is a Bible teacher, or with our church's minister of Christian education. When I need help in counseling, I have access to a professional counselor affiliated with the Narramore Christian Foundation in Phoenix, and my church's family life counselor. I have asked older women who have known the Lord longer than I have to be sure to correct me if they sense I am getting off doctrinally. And or course, the Holy Spirit, as He instructs me from the Word, is my greatest check.

I would encourage a pastor to let women know he is available to help solve problems about doctrine. He might consider leading a session on doctrine at one of the women's leadership training meetings. In those meetings, anyway, we sometimes review the points of our doctrinal stance.

Objection #3: "It is all right for people to win others to the Lord outside the church. But any teaching of these new converts done outside the church is out of the will of God."

Answer: One cannot deny that Scripture (Ephesians 4:11-16) teaches that the local church is the dominant place for teaching and edifying the believer. But it is unrealistic to say that this passage teaches that the local church is the only place where Christians can be taught the Word of God. Daily, the lives of believers touch those who for one reason or another will not attend a Bible-believing church. After these people have been brought to the Lord, and built up somewhat in the faith, their objections to attending church can and do dissipate. Therefore to say that "evangelizing" is the only ministry possible outside the church program, and that "edification" can be done only in the local church program, is to neglect the much-needed teaching of the new Christian.

Many new Christians are committed to their particular church and would not attend a Bible-teaching church until they are taught enough to recognize the difference. As they grow in the Lord they begin to sense the impoverished teaching of one and desire to attend the other.

Jesus had to rebuke His own disciples (Mark 9:38-40) for attempting to stop efforts being done in His name, just because the doers were not immediately under His supervision.

Scripture draws no line around a church building for teaching and spiritual growth. Limiting teaching to the local church — saying, "You must come to church in order to learn" — would mean we can only bring others to Christ as Savior and then tell them they cannot ask any questions. This is totally unnatural. A new believer is full of questions. She can have these questions answered at the women's Bible study and at the same time help it be an evangelistic outreach by bringing interested friends.

Bible studies also reach many women who don't go to church at all but say, "You don't have to go to church to be a Christian." The study groups can be a valuable bridge between the unbeliever or uncommitted Christian, and the local church.

Bible studies are also an asset in towns which have no Bible-believing, Bible-teaching church. The new Christians will begin praying for a pastor! Studies also provide the spiritual "food" for women who teach Sunday school on Sunday mornings, and therefore cannot get to a Sunday school class geared to their own needs.

Objection #4: "The women's Bible study leader would become the pastor to these women."

Answer: Nothing could be further from the truth. The teacher is not trying to act as a pastor. Her purpose is to obey God in teaching the younger women to love their husbands and their children. Her counseling focuses on home problems. The pastor doesn't have the time to counsel all the women in the church. He could be freed of much of this type of work if he would trust the Holy Spirit to do this work through the older godly women. They can deal far better with specialized needs of women, such as revealed by these comments:

"I need some help with my new career as a homemaker. I quit work when I had my baby and now I want to learn how to be a good wife and mother." (Another woman can help a younger one with the day-to-day problems of homemaking.)

"I wish someone would have told me earlier that sex is beautiful. I thought it was ugly and that it was the sin Adam and Eve committed in the Garden. My husband is so happy that I come to Bible study." (Many women feel cheated in loving or believe that sex is "dirty." An older woman who has learned that her body was made for her husband, and his body for her, can share these truths with younger women. I find many women ignorant about God's plan for sex.)

"Since I have been coming to Bible study I am so happy. I am thrilled to know that God has a plan for me as a Christian woman. I now love my home and adore my husband and children. I am no longer filled with self-pity and resentment. God is so good to me." (She learned these attitudes and truths from older women.)

Objection #5: "Bible study will make the women think they know it all and they will attempt to become the spiritual leaders in the homes."

Answer: We do not want women to become spiritual leaders in the home. We encourage them in our Bible study to go home and say to their husbands, "Honey, I learned something new today. I learned that I have been wrong." Wow, do his ears perk up! As she shares an area where God has spoken to her about her own problems, he begins to take an interest in the Bible study. In fact, dozens of women have told me that their *husbands* love our Bible study. I have received many notes over the years from husbands, thanking me for my teaching on the home. One husband sent me a box of chocolates "for telling all those women not to contradict their husbands when they speak." The wives say, "My husband loves you, Naomi, and he hasn't even met you!" Even unsaved men heartily encourage their wives to come. Recently an unsaved husband sent a sealed note via his wife, who had received the Lord on her first day in Bible study. It read: "Please don't ever stop these Bible studies. They have made all the difference in the world in my wife. She is now 100% better toward me and our son. She now loves everyone, even animals, since she found 'it' — this Jesus." He knows Who has changed his wife, and we believe it won't be long before he receives Christ, too.

The problem is not that a wife becomes "too knowledgeable," but that she be coached in proper use of that knowledge. The whole book of Proverbs emphasizes that knowledge without wisdom can be dangerous. The chapter later in this book on counseling tells some ways women can help their husbands become the spiritual leaders in their homes. We give women these suggestions for their home life:

1. Do not read or study your Bible when your husband is home, if it will offend him.

2. Do not talk to him about God if he is "turned off." Let God love him through you. He will begin asking questions.

3. Do not put Scripture verses up all over the house. Learn them in private if necessary. Your life is the best witness there is.

Objection #6: "The instruction in Titus 2:3-5 means that older women should teach by personal example, not by structured classes."

Answer: God's ideal is that every mother and older woman teach her daughter to love and submit to her own husband. But we have slipped from this ideal, as evidenced by the mess many homes now are in. Women tell me that their mother didn't like to cook, so never taught them. They say she was not a good housekeeper (or else a perfectionist) and the family suffered for it. Others sadly say, "My mother was domineering and bossy. I swore I'd never be like that. But I am." Or, "My mother worked outside the home and was always too tired to teach me."

Many older women tell me that they wish they had known when they were younger what they are now learning in Bible study. "I am sure we would not have had such a rough time," they say. Many older women are getting divorces now. What help is that to young marrieds having problems? Many are going to work. Where are the older women who are the "good examples"?

God tells us that older women are to be an "example" to younger women. We all have probably known women who were gracious, godly and kind, whose husbands adored them and whose children grew up to call them "blessed" (Proverbs 31:28). But being an "example" is more than being an actress who can be observed from the third balcony. Young women want the inside tips. They want the specifics on "how." They want some answers. And women's Bible studies provide the right circumstances for sharing these answers. Usually a young woman is more ready to listen to another woman than to her own mother at this time. Hearing and sharing are teaching tools.

Objection #7: "Bible studies become just a place for women to get together and gossip."

Answer: This is untrue of Chris-Town and other Bible studies I am familiar with. Instead there is love and concern for one another. Besides, the time is so well guided and planned that there is really no time for "gossip." Our group coordinator trains the leaders how to deal with the personal problems which might fuel gossip. Gossip could be a problem, I think, in groups which limit study of the Word to a short devotional and leave the rest of the time for idle chatter. But when the Word is taught and applied to lives we find that women evidence in their lives and conversations the favorable qualities known as the "fruit of the spirit" — "love, joy, peace, patience, kindness, goodness, faithfulness, gentleness, self-control." (Galatians 5:22-23 NASB).

Objection #8: "Women should stay at home, not be Bible study gadabouts."

Answer: My answer to this has two parts. First, the job of homemaker and mother is the hardest job in the world. Anyone who has had even one child knows how demanding this job can be. Women find it difficult to be confined to their homes all day, every day, without a break, caring for a family. Many women go to work just to get away from this pressure. One day I stopped to chat with a young mother in a grocery store. I wanted to admire her two children, but before I could say anything she burst out, "I can't wait to go back to work. I can't stand these kids. I'm a nervous wreck." When I invited her to the Bible study, she said, "Oh, no, I'll be going back to work soon." I began telling her how important she was to her children. She replied, "Oh, I have a wonderful woman who will take care of my children. She's had nine of her own." Most of us would hasten to say, "I'm glad that she is going to work for the children's sake." But that is a copout. We older women are to be teaching the younger ones to *love* their families.

It is very important for women to get away from the home one day a week. But I do not believe going to work really solves this need. It usually adds more pressure and demands, which in the end solve very little of the original need for a change of pace. Nothing is more refreshing to a woman than a good day away from the responsibilities of the home. We have found that the Bible study meets these needs:

- It provides good, inexpensive care for the children.
- It provides new friends of her age and interests.
- It provides practical teaching for maintaining a happy home.
- It provides listening and sharing opportunities.
- It provides a growing experience as she finds fulfillment in Christ. She gains a good self-concept and self-confidence as she sees others have similar problems, and as she finds solutions to those problems.
- It provides a place of ministry. She finds great joy in helping someone else.

I found I'd work twice as hard to get things done the rest of the week so that I could have all day Thursday off. If you have never been a young mother, you could not understand how deeply they need this break. In my files are notes from women who said they once tried to commit suicide to escape from the pressures of home life. The nagging question, "What would happen to the children?" was the only thing which kept them from taking their own lives or running away. Then someone brought them to Bible study and they found Jesus. Before long the husbands did, too. Now many of them are serving in a good Bible-believing church, and some help in evening Bible studies. In some cases the husbands are now leading the Bible studies.

I remember one young mother of three who could not go anywhere without her toddlers in tow. She visited our Bible study after several years of deep depression. Although she had a good marriage, the young wife had such a poor self-concept that she trusted no one. She stayed away from church because the ones she had gone to preached "hell-fire and damnation" and she was now convinced that God hated her because of her sins. When she came to Chris-Town she sat and wept as she learned how God loved her. Right there, where she sat, she asked Jesus to forgive her sins and joy flooded her soul. Although she didn't immediately go back to church, she was growing in her love of the Lord and others.

Secondly, we agree that women should not get too busy in church work, Bible studies, conferences and seminars. Because we meet weekly, nine months of the year, we encourage the women to limit attendance at seminars, conferences or studies, and watch their involvement in church work. Otherwise, they would not have the time to put into practice what they are learning about being homemakers. We encourage them to find a good Bible-teaching church and one Bible study which fits their needs. (We do not think everyone should come to Chris-Town.) We encourage them to attend church and a couples' Bible study with their husbands.

I can only repeat my plea: "Husbands and pastors, please let a woman have a day out of the home to learn what kind of woman God would have her be, and share in a deeper Bible study with other women. This will fill her needs for fellowship, understanding and teaching, and she will be a better person for it."

AIM
FOR THE NEED

Gretchen had hardly put the furniture in place in her new home in Wisconsin when it became obvious that God had a role for her in her new town.

"We've been praying for a Bible study here for women or couples," her sister-in-law Sandy, who lived nearby, said excitedly. "Let's do something about it. You have all that insight from your study in Chris-Town."

Sure, Gretchen thought. Chris-Town was unforgettable. But I'm just one woman. And how could I ever start something like *that?*

Barb had moved to Hawaii where her husband wanted to finish his university training and go into full-time Christian work. Soon she felt nudgings that Chris-Town should be transplanted among the palm trees and warm Honolulu breezes. The phone rang. A friend was leaving her husband and was desperate to talk to someone. The doorbell chimed. A bride was tearfully struggling through post-honeymoon jitters. There was another visitor: a woman who'd been brought up in Japan. She was tired of being a "housewife" and wanted to be a "Liberated American Woman" — at the cost of shedding her husband.

That was enough. "Okay, Lord," Barb prayed. "I know there are problems. But how can I start to meet them? Just how do I go about beginning a Bible study?"

Gretchen and Barb, both former Chris-Town study women, were but two of those who have written for advice in beginning a Bible study. As I wrote back I realized that what worked for Chris-Town couldn't be identically duplicated in Wisconsin or Honolulu or wherever God might plant the woman of His choosing. But Proverbs 29:18 says, "Where there is no vision, the people perish." And some basic guidelines needed to be set down.

1. Be willing to let God use and mold you.

Begin today toward becoming the person that God would have you to be. This means you must be a born-again, growing Christian. If you are unsure whether you are a Christian, admit you are a sinner and thank Him for dying for your sins. Invite Him into your life and ask Him to take control. Then:

— Maintain a consistent devotional life of prayer and Bible study. Keep your prayer life fresh through confession of sin. Memorize 1 Corinthians 10:13 and 1 John 1:9. Pray about the people you want to share Christ with. Study the Bible on your own. Memorize Scripture. Take notes on your pastor's sermons. Listen to good Bible-teaching programs on the radio. (Be careful, however, about who you listen to. Some "radio preachers" are actually of cults which distort Christianity.) Read good books about the Bible, but don't let them become a substitute for reading the Bible.

— Let God love others, even the unlovely, through you. You cannot teach love if you are not experiencing it yourself. Be available to others.

— Remember that you are not alone, for Jesus said, "I will never desert you, nor will I ever forsake you" (Hebrews 13:5 NASB).

— As you pray about starting a Bible study, remember, too, that God desires more than you do for people to accept His Son. And remember that only God can give new life. He only asks us as His disciples to "loose them and set them free" (John 11:44, Isaiah 58:6). This comes through sharing God's Word.

2. Involve your husband.

Tell him of your desires to start a study and ask his permission to take on this responsibility. If your husband says no, take this as a "no" from God. Perhaps it is not God's time for you. I remember my husband was at first apprehensive about my involvement in the Bible study. We had four children, all under 5½ and they first of all needed a mother, not — as he feared — someone who would neglect her home for the sake of a Bible study. We talked over the problems of time outside the home, of extra phoning the study would mean. As we worked out suitable rules — for example, no phoning during evenings — my husband approved of the study, releasing me to God for a ministry which the Lord had apparently designed. My home still came first — and still does — but I needed the counsel of my husband to help me maintain that priority.

3. Present the idea to Christian friends you think might be interested in helping you begin a Bible study.

Share with them your burden for others. Show them God's Word, which encourages us to first begin sharing in our own community before reaching into all the world (Acts 1:8). Present the idea that many hands will keep the work from becoming too much for any one person.

Ask them to pray about details of a study (see below). After a time of sharing and prayer, suggest that they talk these things over with their husbands at home, assuring their spouses that the Bible study would not take precedence over the home. Set a day to meet together again and share what God has shown each of you. Your faith will be strengthened as you see how the Lord has led each of you.

Some of the details you need to discuss include:

- Who will teach?
- What should be studied?
- Who will coordinate?
- Where should we meet?
- Where should we have a nursery? (See chapter 5)
- What day of the week should we meet?
- What time should we meet?
- Should we have any "rules"? What?

As they come up, you will need to talk over any other needs. Don't panic. Trust the Lord. Expect great things. Memorize and claim Isaiah 26:3-4:

> *Thou wilt keep him in perfect peace, whose mind is stayed on thee: because he trusteth in thee. Trust ye in the Lord forever: for in the Lord Jehovah is everlasting strength.*

4. Go ahead with God's choice of women.

Even if there are only two of you who agree to start a study, begin laying plans. God doesn't need an impressive number to start His work. To defeat the Midianites He whittled Gideon's army from 32,000 to 300 (Judges 7). For a small Bible study you need only a teacher, a student and the Word.

5. Decide who will teach.

Pray for a Bible teacher if you honestly do not think God wants you to be the teacher. If the Lord wants you to have a Bible study, He will provide a teacher. In almost every group there will be a woman who has more Bible knowledge and has had more experience than the others or has been to a good Bible college. Or, there may be an older woman in your church who really has a love for younger women and a desire to help them come to know the Lord and to obey Him through His Word. Perhaps she is one of your former Sunday school teachers. Or, maybe she led a Bible study years ago, possibly in another state. Maybe your pastor could suggest names. Often the woman who should teach is praying for a study at the same time you are praying for a teacher! Don't be surprised, either, if the pastor encourages you to teach. He may see that this is your spiritual gift and that it needs to be developed.

The person asked to be the teacher may not feel qualified at first to take on the responsibility (and admission she can't do it herself is a good sign!), but urge her to pray about it and consider leading the study at least one semester. If she knows someone else will do the legwork, she may be willing to do the teaching.

It may be best to have one teacher at a time, rather than rotating between different women from week to week. Rotation may result in women choosing their "favorite" speakers and coming only those weeks, thereby missing the continuity of the study.

6. Determine what to teach.

Teach the Bible. Don't be afraid to tackle a book and really dig into it, verse by verse, applying it to homes and lives. I found I could profitably spend a whole year on a single book of Scripture. Many women at Chris-Town say that they remember the year they began in the study by the book of the Bible I was in!

God will honor efforts to teach His word. He says His Word "shall not return unto me void, but it shall accomplish that which I please" (Isaiah 55:11). You may think that the women would prefer a study that passes over the surface of various subjects. But if you are diligent in studying and teaching a book of the Bible, you will see more growth and change in their lives.

A pastor can recommend study helps or commentaries to help with lesson preparation. But these should not replace prayerful study of the Word itself.

Women are interested in learning. You'll quickly find, too, that their interests are diverse. Once when I asked, "What do you want to study?", I received these answers:

● "I'd like to investigate the debate of creation and evolution."

● "What commandments is Jesus speaking about when He says, 'He that loveth me keepeth my commandments'?"

● "I'm interested in the virgin birth, predestination, and why blood sacrifice is necessary."

● "I'm interested in studying about prayer."

● "I want to know how to 'love they neighbor.' Help!"

● "I would like to know Jesus in a real way. This will help me in my home life and in my discouragements."

● "I would like to study the Old Testament."

● "I am new this year. I haven't studied the Bible since I was a child, but I want to learn it so I can be a better wife and mother. So I guess I just want a basic Bible study."

● "The book of Revelation troubles me. I don't understand it. Also, when the apostles gave instructions to the church, did they include us? Why are there so many conflicting doctrinal teachings? I would enjoy a study of doctrines and why we know which one is right."

● "I would like a study of the Holy Spirit and how He relates to my life."

● "I believe God wants me to teach the high school girls at church. I've always taught seven-year-olds and I'm scared to death about teaching teenagers. But I took 25 high schoolers to camp and after counseling with them I see their many needs. I want to teach them God's Word to strengthen their lives."

● "I need to study the Bible so I can answer my son's many questions."

● "I want to find peace of mind as Jesus taught we could have."

Obviously, a single lecture cannot meet all these questions and needs at once, but watch for opportunities to include them in your study. This is also where the second-hour study groups are an advantage (see chapter 6). If your Bible study has 15 women or more, you should seriously consider adding small second-hour group studies relating to the women's specific needs.

Here, too, as in the main lecture, some believe a teacher should develop her own material. Study guides, of course, are available on various books of the Bible. But many of our more mature teachers prefer not to rely on these and come up with their own question-and-answer approach to teaching.

If you consider a study guide, check with a knowledgeable person before buying a whole stack. I have been satisfied with the scholarship and preparation of study guides put out by The Navigators, Campus Crusade for Christ, and Inter-Varsity Christian Fellowship, to name only a few. These may be ordered through Christian bookstores or through the organization's headquarters.

7. Decide who will serve as "coordinator."

The teacher will have enough to do preparing her lessons. Have someone else pick up the loose ends, such as inviting women, arranging for nursery facilities and extra chairs, etc. If you are starting this study by yourself, ask God to send you a woman who would love to help this way. As your group grows, the coordinator may assign some specific helpers for three major areas (see chapter 5 for more details on these helpers):

a. Nursery chairman — to arrange for babysitters and make sure there are enough facilities for children.

b. Hostess — to fix coffee and coordinate who brings cookies or similar snacks. You may want to put a cup on the table labeled "Donations for Coffee" to help defray expenses.

c. Greeters — to greet newcomers, give them name tags and introduce them around.

8. Decide where to meet.

You probably will start by meeting in your home, but there is no limit to the variety of places women's Bible studies can be held. In small towns you probably would stay in a home; in cities you may move to a hall. Other possibilities are townhouse or trailer court recreation rooms, shopping mall auditoriums, bank auditoriums or church buildings.

9. Determine a place for the nursery.

Avoid keeping the children and the study in the same house. It's too distracting and when children realize their mothers are just around the corner, they may demand mama's time. Try to find two homes near each other so one home can be the nursery and one the Bible study meeting place. Or, see about using a church nursery.

Call local churches for names of women who sit in the church nursery Sunday mornings. They are your top candidates for Bible study sitters. Teen-age family sitters, of course, would be in school. They could, however, be used in the summer if you meet then. For the older children, seek a Christian who enjoys telling Bible stories and teaching songs to youngsters.

As I mentioned, our first study began in my home. The home of

Jackie, my coordinator, was next door and her third bedroom became the "nursery." We obtained several cribs for that room, assigning one sitter to the babies. The other sitter stayed with the older children outside, or in Jackie's family room.

10. Set a regular day for the study.

You will have to mutually decide the best day of the week to meet. We found Thursdays best because that still left us Friday to get ready for the activities of the weekend. We voted against Monday because it was too soon after Sunday and also wash day for most women. Tuesday was out because it seemed too soon in the week to have a lesson prepared. Wednesday was busy preparing for Pioneer Girls or other church involvements. Friday was voted out as too close to the weekend.

11. Assign a time for the study.

We tried many different time schedules. We learned early that some women will come late no matter how late in the morning you begin. With real desire and a bit of planning they too could make an earlier starting hour unless their husbands leave late for work. As your study settles down into a pattern you may want to adopt the schedule we found best:

8:00 — Coordinator arrives to set things up. I arrive shortly after to set up for the teaching time. Prepare overhead projector, be sure microphone is on and a light is on the podium. I have a prayer time with the helpers who come early to set things up. That way I am free later to visit.

8:30 — Helpers arrive for the book table, guest table, coffee table, etc. (See chapter 5 for description of their duties.)

8:45 — Prayer time. This includes prayer for guests, for the study and for unsaved husbands.

9:00 — Coffee and fellowship time. Women browse at book and tape tables, if you have any.

9:15 SHARP! — Begin when you say you will. Start with singing. It will prepare both the speaker and the women for the message. Fay, Chris-Town's songleader for a number of years, is a very special person who can radiate God's love as she leads the music. (This and her loving attitude help new women feel close to her. So, she also assists in the second-hour guest group.) We sing contemporary choruses which deeply touch the hearts of the women. Many of the newer songs are taken directly from Scripture, and by the time we finish singing my heart is so full that I can hardly wait to get to the podium to teach.

9:30 — Speaker. Occasionally, too, we will have a solo or short testimony from one of the women.

10:20 — Announcements by the coordinator. She keeps them as brief as possible, checking them off a list as she gives them. She also acknowledges guests by having them stand. This is the time, too, to take a free-will offering or to defray expenses of the sitters, building rent or study papers.

10:30 — Small group studies (see chapter 6 for details).

11:30 — Close.

11:30-1:00 (once a month) — Potluck luncheon.

12. Go ahead with that first study.

Invite your friends and neighbors to your home. Have coffee ready and some goodies attractively arranged. Share your own testimony or ask someone who has come to know the Lord and whose home is happy to tell what it means to be obedient to God. One good starting place for a first-time testimony is Genesis 2:18. Tell some of the things you have been learning in relation to your husband, as you apply that verse to your life. Afterwards, allow time for discussion. If women talk before the explanation of God's solutions, the conversation may get dragged down in the world's solutions. Suggest homework such as a memory verse and an assignment. Propose, for example, that all the women really respond to their husbands this week — like going with him someplace he asks, even if it's just to get gas for the car.

Another possible way to start a Bible study is to have the teacher share a short Bible study on the home and about God's love. Genesis 2:18-25 and 1 Peter 3:1-6 are good passages for this.

Be loving, friendly and caring. The women will not come unless they see their needs can be met. This includes love. Do not push them to receive the Lord as their Savior. The Holy Spirit will convict them in His own time.

During the following week, pray daily by name for each woman who came. Trust the Lord to use His Word in the women's lives.

Exactly how you will conduct that first study will vary according to your situation. One Chris-Town "alumna" mentioned at the beginning of this chapter, Gretchen, decided to follow the Chris-Town format for her study. Her coordinator turned out to be her sister-in-law, Sandy. They decided to share the teaching load, however, so Gretchen taught the first hour, sharing what the Bible says about the home beginning in 1 Peter 3. Then Sandy led the group of 20 women during the second hour in a study from one of the guides prepared by The Navigators. They had made sure there would be enough guides on hand for each woman there. That first day, too, they had someone give her testimony relating how God can and does change lives.

As your group grows, invite the women to help with coffee, nursery, luncheons and so on. They will feel more like it is their class. The potluck luncheons may become a special binding agent. Each woman should bring one dish of food (salad, meat, vegetable or dessert); the hostess or treasurer will provide paper plates, coffee and tea. We asked that mothers with toddlers prepare sack lunches (leaving out any messy foods) for the little ones to eat with their sitters. Mothers of babies take time out to feed them and then return from the nursery for lunch.

Some good ideas for your first study may also be gleaned from the excellent booklet, "Evangelistic Speaking and Entertaining," put out by Campus Crusade for Christ.

13. Insist on two "game" rules.

a. Request that the women refrain from talking specifically about their church backgrounds. Tell them that you want your Bible study to center around the Person of Christ and not on churches. This will alleviate the tensions of denominational differences.

If your Bible study is a church-related study, be careful not to become ingrown or cliquish. Don't talk "church" or you'll lose your guests.

b. Remind the women not to go home and tell their husbands all the things the husbands should be "doing." Reinforce the truth of 1 Peter 3:1 (NASB): "In the same way, you wives, be submissive to your own husbands so that even if any of them are disobedient to the word, they may be won without a word by the behavior of their wives." Urge them to substitute "lectures" with the admission, "Honey, I learned something today . . . that I was wrong."

14. Welcome problems as opportunities for prayer.

Don't panic when your first problem comes. Trust the Lord. Let the group pray about needs — then they can rejoice when the answer comes. You will make mistakes. But God can overrule.

Ask some of your older Christian friends to pray for the group and especially for the teacher. Many precious elderly women have prayed for me. One named Maude, in her mid-80s, has prayed daily for me the past few years. And — she still attends Bible study almost every week. Maude is a woman with many spiritual children, including Louise, 20 years her junior, who leads our guest group (see chapters 2 and 6).

Remember, you are not alone in your problems. Claim the promise of Philippians 4:6-7 — that you should be anxious "for nothing; but in every thing by prayer and supplication with thanksgiving let your requests be made known unto God. And the peace of God, which passeth all understanding, shall keep your hearts and minds through Christ Jesus."

15. Be alert to God's surprises.

The Lord may open up the opportunity for a Bible study in a way you never expected. This was true of Judy, who really learned how God can bless a submissive wife when her husband proposed a move to another part of the state. Hers was not a church-going family, so she found special strength and encouragement through the Chris-Town studies. Leaving was the last thing she wanted to do. But she was in for a surprise.

"Honey," her husband said one night. "When we get settled let's find a church together and start going."

Judy's joy was quickly checked by apprehension, however, when her husband favored a particular church which Judy felt would not help them spiritually. She genuinely wondered if God could place her in a situation which she feared would hamper their spiritual lives. On the other hand, she knew she had to be a submissive wife.

Lovingly explaining her objections to that particular church, she told her husband, "If you really think this is where we should go, I'll follow your leading."

They joined the church.

"My attitude left much to be desired," Judy recalls. "I felt like I was just treading water, not willing to get involved in the church, not really going anywhere, and hoping that the Lord would move us on somewhere else quickly. Then our pastor's wife invited me to their women's evening circle. I really dragged my feet and didn't want to go. I stuck a handful of 'Four Spiritual Laws' booklets into my purse before leaving for the meeting. My attitude was sour. But on the way, God spoke to me about my grumbling. Before I went up the walkway, I had to confess my lack of faith in His plan for my life.

"I wasn't the only new person at the meeting. There were several, so each of us was asked to give our name and tell something exciting about ourselves. I took that as my cue to share how Jesus became real in my life.

In a brief way I shared the Gospel as I had first heard it through the Four Spiritual Laws.

"To my surprise, they were receptive and asked if I had any of those 'Four Spiritual Laws' I had mentioned in my talk. I passed around my copies and read through the whole booklet. I went home that night rejoicing!

"I continued attending that circle and later was asked to lead in a Bible study. I have seen women accept Christ and really take root and grow. Seeds are being planted in many other lives. What is happening in my life and in the church would take pages to describe. I can only praise the Lord!"

OTHER TYPES OF STUDIES

God can use and reach women through other types of Bible studies, too. One of the young women from the Chris-Town study decided to hold a children's Bible study for her neighborhood children. Not only did the children love it, but some of the mothers called and asked the leader what she "had" that they didn't. As a result, three mothers began coming to the Chris-Town study.

You may also want to reach your office friends or teens. If so, here are some practical suggestions for each type of study:

OFFICE BIBLE STUDIES

Many women who work desire to get into a Bible study, and office Bible studies also provide a tremendous opportunity to reach your associates in the business world with the love of God. Believers in secular employment need fellowship to cope with the pressure and temptations of the business world. Psalm 1 tells believers not to counsel with unbelievers and this is difficult when believers are with unbelievers all week long.

When? A day of the week is the best and usually during the lunch hour. You will find that others from other offices will hear about your group and want to share with you in the study of God's Word.

Where? Ask about conference rooms. They are usually available to groups upon request.

How? If men are involved, the study should be led by a man. It is important that he know the Lord as his Savior and walk in obedience to all he knows in the Word. If the group is women only, then a woman should lead.

I believe it is best to have a discussion group using guides such as those put out by Navigators or Campus Crusade for Christ. Your local Christian bookstore may have suggestions for materials. These guides allow others to study and participate, and share what they are learning. This too would help prevent the study from becoming a lecture. Any time you can get someone to find the answers from himself, you will have been a better "teacher." (See the chapter on small groups for suggestions on teaching techniques.) Encourage those who come to memorize a verse a week. Also, as your group becomes acquainted and more comfortable with one another, they will want to share prayer requests and pray for each other. Do not ask anyone to pray until you know they are ready to pray and feel comfortable with the group.

TEENS' BIBLE STUDIES

Who? Gather the teens of your neighborhood together or the gang from your teen's friends from school. Or, invite the teens from your church group. Teens love to get together. Invitation can be by word-of-mouth.

Where? Have the study where teens can relax. Chairs where they have to sit up straight are *out!* Try places like a basement, garage, family room, around the pool or in a vacant lot.

What to serve? Teens love food. Any kind! Let each sign up to bring something. Chips, dip, cookies are always winners. Wiener roasts are especially fun. Punch is less expensive than pop. Food is a great incentive to come. Be wise!

How to lead? Teens, like all of us, love to share what they know, and they want to ask questions. If you do not know the answer, suggest that you all go home and study it out and come back the next week to share what you learned. This would be a good time to show them how to use a commentary or concordance.

I suggest that you use the same booklet for the teens as for the adults: the Navigators' Ten Basic Study books. Do not talk down to teens. They are sharp and want to be treated as such. Sit in a circle, not rows (heaven forbid!). Use a table or sit on the floor. Let the teens bring their own Bibles. They will have many different translations but you will find that they do not differ as greatly as we have been led to think. The teens are so thrilled to find out that they can have a personal relationship with God through the Lord Jesus Christ. They are delighted also to find that they can find answers to their questions as they study. If you get into something controversial, tell them that the group is there to find out what the Bible says about the subject. Be sure to have them read the verses before and after the verse in question when there is a problem. Trust the Holy Spirit to be the teacher. The Lord gives you wisdom. Whatever you do, don't put anyone down because they differ from you. You might even say at a time like that, "We all have differences, but let's disagree agreeably." You'll find in time as you study you all will come to a better understanding of God's Word.

When? Any time of the year is good. During the school session you could have the study right after school or in the evening, depending on your particular situation. We enjoyed having our eighth grade Bible study after school from 4 to 5:30. The kids played basketball (boys against girls — they love that!). Then we had refreshments (cold punch and cookies) followed by a sit-down game for a few minutes. Then we all opened our Bibles and the Navigator books (we had extra Bibles for those who forgot or had none). I began with the question we had left off on the week before, and we began to share what we had learned and what we didn't understand. What a joy to see 20 to 30 teens each week studying the Word of God. Many have expressed their thanks, these many years later.

In the summers we'd start with swim parties. Often we went for picnics. This also gave the fellows and gals a chance to be together with those "chaperones" whom they really didn't mind having because they knew we loved them. My husband loved the kids and also led some of the studies. He helped plan and participated in picnics.

Teen Bible studies are a great help to teens who do not have much to do in the summers. There are so many things our children can get into which are not good: drugs, sex, stealing and so on. We who know the Lord must stem the tide. God has given us the awesome responsibility of reaching a lost world with the Good News. You have "the world" at your door in those around you. Don't be afraid to tell them about Christ. They love anyone who loves them. Be interested in them. Be positive. Smile. Call them by name. Whether they come to know Jesus or not, may depend on you.

> *Where there is no vision, the people (teens) perish. (Proverbs 29:18, my addition)*

CHILDREN'S BIBLE STUDIES

Who? Invite the neighborhood children from everywhere: from church, school and, or course, the neighborhood. You may want to invite children from a particular grade or grades at school. Call or send out invitations. Word of mouth is good, but some parents would want more information. You may wish to contact several Christian mothers for help. Don't be discouraged if it starts slow.

When? During the school year you could meet after school, maybe from 4 to 5. During the summer you could meet on a week day, morning or afternoon. You may want the children to bring cookies for refreshments. (You also may want to check into Child Evangelism classes. See your phone directory for an office near you. See also Bible Club Movement people in your area for suggestions and helps. Both of these groups train their own leaders.)

Where? Meet on the patio or in the family room, a basement room, or any place where children can be comfortable. If you use a living room and it is rainy, you may care to have them slip off their shoes at the door.

What to teach? Your Bible stores have all the material you could want. For small children, you could use flannelgraph to teach the life of Christ or the biography of Paul or Moses. Your heart will thrill as you see these little ones come to know the Lord and begin to grow in His love.

Why have children's classes? Classes for children are important because children need Jesus, too. It is better to come to know Christ as a child and have your whole life to live for Him. Many of the women in our Bible study came to know Christ as a child and God kept a hunger for His Word in their hearts. They now are teaching their children to love the Lord, too. If you have children, you would be the ideal person to teach. If you are a grandma, you could be an even better choice to teach because all children love a "gramma" and many are hundreds of miles away from their own. Don't be afraid that they will ruin your furniture. If you are loving and strict, they will honor your wishes. Have them sit on the floor, if you prefer.

Try having the children take turns, one or two a week, reviewing the flannel graph story from the week before. This helps reinforce the lesson and also helps the children to feel more a part. You might be training a future Bible teacher.

You may also want to give rewards to those who bring the most children. We used a "net" and put cardboard "fishes" in it for each new one brought, and the name of the one who brought them. Then we gave a prize to the one who caught the most "fish." Jesus said, "Follow me, and I will make you fishers of men."

At the end of the summer or "year" you may want to invite the parents so that they can see what the children have learned. When I did this, I let the children do most of the storytelling. They marched in singing a song they had learned and interspersed the evening with songs. The children had brought the dessert so it was not costly for anyone. We held this "party" in the back yard.

"It is more blessed to give than to receive" (Acts 20:35). There comes a time when we need to take time to give out what we know rather than look for another Bible study where someone can lead us.

THE TEACHER

Edith had no Bible school training, but her heart was saturated with the Word of God. Ever since the age of 16, when she accepted Christ in Louise's and my teen Bible club, she had eagerly studied the Word. Even marriage and the birth of three sons couldn't slow her down.

Her excitement for Bible study infected her neighbors and soon they came each week to study Scriptures. They brought friends — and more friends — and in time her living room was wall-to-wall women. They switched meeting places to a bank auditorium and finally to a local Bible church. From a handful Edith's group grew to 150.

Pretty, red-haired Peggy was married to a professor at Arizona College of the Bible. Her first priority as a young wife was maintaining a pleasant home and caring for their two-year-old daughter. Thursdays she saved to attend the Chris-Town Women's Bible study. It was a welcome break from "home" in a mobile home court.

But Peggy was alert to the needs of women living around her and decided to invite some in to study the Bible. They came back — and this young woman who thought she was too young to teach found herself with a regular class.

Who chose Edith to teach? God did — by putting the desire in her heart and preparing her to communicate. Who chose Peggy? God did — by burdening her for her neighbors and rekindling her enthusiasm for studying the Word through the Chris-Town study.

When God looks for teachers, he looks for faithfulness, not greatness. I Corinthians 4:2 says, "Moreover it is required in stewards, that a man be found faithful." God looks for availability, then takes care of the matter of ability. He looks for someone through whom He can show His great power: "For the eyes of the Lord run to and fro throughout the whole earth, to show himself strong in the behalf of them whose heart is perfect toward him" (2 Chronicles 16:9).

THE TEACHER AS A PERSON

A woman who teaches the Bible must know its Author, God Himself, through a personal relationship with His Son, Jesus Christ. Along with this, she must be committed to obeying Him and to continuously learning about Him.

She should be one who knows what women's needs are. She must be able to relate to those needs and bring others gently to the One who can meet them.

Although helpful, it is not necessary for a woman to have a diploma from Bible college or a seminary degree to qualify as a Bible teacher. She can become knowledgeable of Scripture through personal daily study. She can take notes on sermons and lessons of a Bible-teaching pastor. Her classroom can be well-chosen Bible broadcasts such as "Through the Bible" (Dr. J. Vernon McGee), "The Know Your Bible Hour" (Dr. John Mitchell), "The Radio Bible Class" (Richard DeHaan), and "Back to the Bible" (Dr. Theodore H. Epp). At her Christian book store she can find good magazines and books about the Bible.

Her prayerful study of the Word should expand her spiritual horizons and deepen her walk with God. The result will be a life manifesting the fruits of the Spirit (Galatians 5:22-23), a humble and teachable spirit, and a desire to share the Word with others.

Many Christians are like the Dead Sea — all intake and no outgo. They're spiritually stagnant. If our lives are to overflow with God's blessings, then we need to share, to pour out as well as take in. This "pouring out" involves a conscious effort, coupled with prayer to God to be able to relate Scriptures to everyday life, applying them to problems. If there is no application, the message will change no lives. Well-developed material and a flawless delivery will be useless if they affect only the head and not the heart.

Someone once said that the mark of a great teacher is to begin where his students are and bring them to where he wants them to be. Jesus taught like this. He spoke of the things the people knew — the lilies, sheep, vines, brides and bridegrooms — and went from there into deeper truths. This is where the women's Bible study teacher must start. Her life must be so steeped in the Word of God that she knows personally its practical implications for living, and is able to relate those truths to where people live.

God gives gifts to his children for the work of the ministry (see Romans 12:1-16, 1 Corinthians 12:1-31 and Ephesians 4:1-16). These gifts fall into two main categories: the serving gifts and the speaking gifts. These gifts do not usually come "full-blown." They are in embryonic form and must be developed. This development takes much time and patience. It takes trial and error — as learning anything does.

Many think that good Bible teachers have always taught that well. Nothing could be further from the truth. Everyone who teaches had his or her time of nervousness, apprehension and fear.

Many Christians I meet do not know what their spiritual gift is. Because they cannot speak like a particular seasoned teacher, many feel they are not gifted to teach. I believe that one of the best ways to determine your spiritual gift is by asking God to show you, and then by asking yourself which area — speaking or serving — you prefer to work. If you have a deep desire to teach others, even though you do not feel qualified, you may move in that direction. Expect to begin slowly, making some mistakes. But also expect God to bless as you teach His Word, for He has said that His Word "shall not return unto me void, but it shall accomplish that which I please, and it shall prosper in the thing whereto I sent it" (Isaiah 55:11).

God is more eager to show you your gift than you are to know what it is and to use it. Be sure to seek the Giver of gifts rather than the gifts themselves. God has said it is possible to have a gift without love, but to use a gift without love is to nullify its value (see 1 Corinthians 13:1-3).

As you acquire knowledge and understanding and share this with friends, do not be ashamed to admit that you do not know everything. Be willing to say, "I don't know the answer to that question. Let's go home and find the answer."

A teacher must always be teachable and never get to the place where she thinks she knows it all. I thing this teachable spirit is the most significant quality I've seen in the women who went out from the Chris-Town study and started studies of their own. Desiring to be teachable, they were humble. They were obedient. They were willing to face obstacles and difficult times with sweetness and courage. They kept in the Word.

Scripture tells us about qualities every Christian leader should develop. Here are 13 which are as true for a teacher as for anyone else in Christian leadership:

1. Trust the Lord (Proverbs 3:5-6)
2. Be faithful (1 Corinthians 4:2)
3. Study to be approved of God (2 Timothy 2:15)
4. Be ready to give an answer to anyone who asks (1 Peter 3:15).

5. Be filled with the Spirit (Ephesians 5:18)
6. Evidence the fruit of the Spirit (Galatians 5:22-23)
7. Be prayerful (Philippians 4:6-7)
8. Be thankful (1 Thessalonians 5:18)
9. Be friendly (Proverbs 18:24)
10. Be humble (1 Peter 5:6)
11. Be forgiving (Ephesians 4:31-32)
12. Be loving (1 Corinthians 13:4-7)
13. Acknowledge that it is His power in you and His life in you that will make the Bible study successful (John 15:5, 2 Chronicles 16:9 and Colossians 1:27-29).

THE TEACHER'S PURPOSE

A teacher's primary purpose is to glorify God. An important way she does this is by reaching women where they are, helping them to know the Lord and to personally apply the Word of God to their homes and lives.

A young woman recently remarked to me, "Through our study in Proverbs this year I have learned that God thinks women are important. Now I am more fulfilled because I am learning that God wants me to be at home – and, I am happy being there."

Another said, "I'm so thrilled to have found a Bible study where the teachers understands what I am going through."

Besides ministering to women where they are, a Bible study should be a tool of teaching them to help others. We are under obligation, as Paul communicated to Timothy: "And the things which you have heard from me in the presence of many witnesses, these entrust to faithful men, who will be able to teach others also" (2 Timothy 2:2 NASB). God says older women are to teach the younger women "to love their husbands, to love their children, to be sensible, pure, workers at home, kind, being subject to their own husbands, that the word of God may not be dishonored" (Titus 2:3-4 NASB). A woman's behavior is either a credit or a discredit to her home. How she behaves as a wife and homemaker is a reflection not only on herself and her family, but upon God.

A TEACHER'S PREPARATION

The most exciting part about preparing for teaching is knowing that we're not in it alone. We may gather the material, but the Holy Spirit is there to illumine the meaning and then bring it to memory (2 Timothy 2:15 and John 14:26). The hour we're supposed to teach, He sends the courage to put one foot in front of the other, walk to the podium and open our mouths:

> *I can do all things through Christ which strengtheneth me. (Philippians 4:13)*

> *Before I formed thee in the belly I knew thee; and before thou camest forth out of the womb I sanctified thee, and I ordained thee a prophet unto the nations. Then said I, Ah, Lord God! behold, I cannot speak: for I am a child. But the Lord said unto me, Say not, I am a child: for thou shalt go to all that I shall send thee, and whatsoever I command thee thou shalt speak. Be not afraid of their faces: for I am with thee to deliver thee, saith the Lord. Then the Lord put forth his hand, and touched my mouth. And the Lord said unto me, Behold, I have put my words in thy mouth. (Jeremiah 1:5-9)*

Dare to trust the Lord to illuminate your mind as you study the Bible. Read the passage, re-read it, and, like a cow chewing her cud, "chew it" even when you can't spend time actually studying. Ask, what does it say? What does it mean? As questions come to your mind, write them down and find some answers. You'll need a good concordance, a Bible dictionary and a Bible handbook for an overall view. Helpful as handbooks are *Halley's Bible Handbook* (Zondervan) and Henrietta Mears' *What the Bible Is All About* (Regal Books). The questions you have about a passage or book are probably the questions someone else would have. As the passage comes clear and meaningful to you, you will be better able to communicate it to others.

For example, suppose the passage you are dealing with discusses faith. You could look up the word "faith" in your concordance. Ask these questions of each reference you read:

1. What is faith?
2. Where does it come from?
3. Who may have it?
4. How do they get it?
5. When may I have faith?
6. How is it to be used?
7. Why do we need faith?

Be sure to read the entire section where that verse is found so you understand it in its context. This will also guard against misapplication and false teaching — problems which come about when people lift verses from their moorings. After — and only after — you have studied and gleaned all you can about a subject, then turn to a good commentary. Your thorough study from the Bible will help you say with confidence, "God says. . . ." rather than "So-and-so says. . . ."

Always apply the Word to yourself as you read. Make it personal. The Bible is not always "to" you, but all the Bible is written "for" you, for your learning.

It is important , too, to be aware of the time period when various parts of the Bible were written. For example, in Luke 24:29 Christ said He would send the Holy Spirit and told the disciples they should "tarry ye in the city of Jerusalem, until ye be endued with power from on high." Remember that Christ had not yet ascended, and He had to do this before sending the Spirit. However, some people today erroneously apply this instruction to the contemporary church, believing people must tarry and wait for the Holy Spirit to come into their lives. They pray and agonize, hoping for an "experience" that will assure them of the presence of the Holy Spirit in their lives. But the Scripture written to our situation — the church which grew up after the ascension of Christ and the sending of the Holy Spirit at Pentecost in Jerusalem — says that the Holy Spirit comes into our lives at the time each person receives Christ. 1 Corinthians 12:13 says, "For by one Spirit are we all baptized into one body, whether we be Jews or Gentiles, whether we be bond or free; and have been all made to drink into one Spirit." 1 Corinthians 6:19-20 says those who have been bought with a price (those who have accepted the salvation secured through Christ's death) are "the temple of the Holy Ghost which is in you." Acts 10:44 records how a group of Gentiles received the Holy Spirit at the time they believed: "While Peter yet spake these words, the Holy Ghost fell on all them which heard the word." These passages are just one illustration of how important the context of time period is in interpreting Scripture.

Keep your study Bible-centered. Don't parrot the commentaries. God is able to use His Word to change lives. Hebrews 4:12 says, "the word of God is quick, and powerful, and sharper than any two-edged sword, piercing even to the dividing asunder of soul and spirit, and of the joints and marrow, and is a discerner of the thoughts and intents of the heart."

As you prepare your study, remember the needs of your women. Are all of them Christians? Are all of them unsaved? Is your group a mixture? Pray that you'll be able to speak to the needs of both. Don't place yourself above your women. We are all sinners saved by God's grace. And, we are all learning. Remember, the ultimate response belongs to Him: "I have planted, Apollos watered; but God gave the increase (1 Corinthians 3:6).

One last suggestion: keep files for your studies. Fill a file box or drawer with manila folders, labeled by book of the Bible or by topic. Use the folders to keep studies you have already given or to gather material for future studies. You also may want to keep all your notes on paper of the same size for ease in transferring from one notebook to another.

THE TEACHER'S PRESENTATION

I believe a verse-by-verse study of books of the Bible is the most profitable way to study Scripture. By no means is it the only method, but I have found it a sharp sword in dealing with our lives and homes. Some of my women remark, laughing, "Naomi, you could take any book of the Bible and teach about the home from it." I suppose this isn't too far from the truth, because Scripture brims with truth for every area of our lives. But I usually select books of the Bible which are more readily applicable to our daily lives. Some of my favorites are John, Romans, 1 Peter, 1 and 2 Corinthians, Philippians, Hebrews, the Pentateuch (the first five books of the Old Testament, especially Genesis) and Proverbs. You may think when you start a book that you'll finish it long before the year is up. But you'll find, if you truly dig into it, verse by verse, that you'll wish you had more than a year to finish it.

To start a Bible study you may begin in a book which contains a truth which stirred you to Bible study. If the Lord used a particular verse or chapter to meet some need in your life, you can be certain that someone else could profit from it, too. Don't be as concerned about the delivery as about the content.

The lecture method. By choice when I began the women's Bible study years ago I sat down *with* the women. But when the study grew beyond all expectations, I found my sitting days were over. A group discussion became impractical; a lecture became the most efficient way of imparting the Word. A lecture meant more women could hear the Word. But it also meant there could be no verbal interaction.

We solved this dilemma by dividing the study time. The first hour I would lecture; the second hour, the women divided into small groups and there had the necessary interaction.

I believe there are advantages to the lecture hour for a large group. One of the most important involves women who come bitter or hostile to God or Christianity in general. During the lecture hour they can listen to the Word without the opportunity to challenge what they hear. The Holy Spirit can use that first hour in a powerful way to begin healing deep hurts. As it is expressed in Psalm 46:10: "Be still, and know that I am God." By the time the study opens for discussion (in small groups, if the main group is large), these women will be thoughtfully considering what they have heard. They will be less likely to vent their anger on the group.

Close the lecture with a clear presentation of the Gospel, a practical assignment drawn from the lesson, a Bible reading assignment and possibly a memory verse. Let God lead.

After the lesson a teacher should be available to the women. Don't be a mystery figure who arrives late and leaves early. Mix with the women and get to know them. Share their problems and joys. You might ask them to write on 3x5 cards what kinds of questions they have about God's Word and their personal lives. Weave these needs into your studies, and your lessons will be more powerful. Take time to pray with women – the babes in Christ as well as the older ones who are having difficulties as leaders. Encourage them. All of us have problems. But we need to be turned to the One who wants our problems turned over to Him – and Who offers victory.

The discussion method. Use questions as a teaching technique for a small group study. Questions have several advantages. First, they stimulate thinking and encourage concentration, "bringing into captivity every thought to the obedience of Christ" (2 Corinthians 10:5). For example, in a study of Genesis 7 you could note that God told Noah to "come" into the ark. Now form this fact into a question, asking the class, "What significance is there in God's saying, 'Come thou' instead of 'Go on in, Noah'?"

Second, questions help correct false ideas. I grew up thinking that Noah was in the ark 40 days and 40 nights. Actually it was more than a year. So in a study about the Flood, one could ask, "How long was Noah in the Ark?" They will have to hunt to find out!

Third, questions stimulate profitable discussion. Many discussion sessions stagnate because they become sounding boards for human ideas. You can tell when a class degenerates to this point because most of the comments will be preceded by "I think . . ." Encourage the women to center the discussion around what God says and how it can be applied to the problem. For example, in asking "What was wrong with the fig leaves?", turn their attention to Genesis 3:7 and 3:21.

Fourth, questions emphasize a fact to build on later. The question, "What was wrong with Cain's offering?", will be a foundation for the rest of the Pentateuch and in fact the entire Biblical story of sacrifice and redemption.

If your personal well of questions runs dry, ask the women to compose three questions for the lesson, either a question not covered or one they think would be a good one for class discussion. You may discover some deep thinking by one who may not be very talkative yet has something to contribute. This also helps you evaluate your effectiveness in covering the subject.

One way to close the discussion lesson, apart from the usual way of "Now let's review," would be to leave the women with questions. For example, when studying Genesis 37 and 38 the leader could ask, "What sequence of events led up to Joseph's arrival in Egypt?" The question encourages them to go back over the chapters about Joseph's early life. This could be part of the homework. It is important to leave with them some leading questions to study for the next week's lesson.

If you encounter snags in your Bible study, look to others for help. Ask a Bible-believing pastor or Sunday school teacher to recommend a good commentary — or several — so that you might glean from what God has shown other godly teachers. But don't become trapped by commentaries. I remember hearing of a little, older woman who said, "I just love to read my Bible because it throws so much light on the commentary!" When you open the Bible itself you are saying, in effect, "The Bible is the authority for its own interpretation."

Application of scripture. Charles G. Finney, a well-known Bible expositor, believed that Bible teaching without moral application could be worse than no teaching at all. And that's true. We can hear a Bible story over and over, but unless its principles are applied to our lives, we might as well not have heard it at all. The women in your study will want to know how something penned onto papyrus thousands of years ago can be meaningful to them in the 20th century. A teacher must help the class to see Scripture as practical. For example, in studying about Abraham we learn that his son Isaac was called the "Son of Promise." The question could be asked, "What three promises has God given you in His Word, that you have claimed?" Ask the class what timeless truth is illustrated by the Bible passage. For example, Abraham's willingness to sacrifice Isaac in obedience to God shows us how we, too, must obey God's Word, trusting Him to work out the results according to His promise. Ask class members, "Can you think of something God is asking you to obey Him in which is difficult for you — and yet He has given a promise to you if you trust Him?"

True application, though, does not come from a set of principles arrived at during study. It is something that must come through the ministry of the Holy Spirit. He must help a person transfer the knowledge to the heart. Psalm 127:1 says, "Except the Lord build the house, they labor in vain that build it." As we build our houses — as we build up women through Bible studies — we must be careful that we use the right construction material: the applied Word of God.

THE TEACHER'S PROBLEMS

A teacher is a learner. And that includes learning from mistakes. Little things will "teach" you as you begin. Your notes may drop, but the next week you'll be sure to put your papers on the podium more securely. There may be interference from outside; next week, you'll be sure to close the door. You will learn what works, and what doesn't.

One of my biggest discouragements was thinking, after I got home from Bible study, about how I had trouble remembering a reference or how I stumbled over a word. Sometimes a woman would come up to me after class and ask, "What was that third thing you said you would share with us?" But it was too late to go back and tell the class that day. That was when God gave me Donna. She would sit on the front row, praying for me and quietly and unobtrusively helping with a word or reference. If I forgot a point she would graciously say, "Naomi, what was the third point?" I felt much better knowing that if I forgot something important or unknowingly said the wrong thing, it could be cleared up before the hour ended.

Fear might be your problem. That has been my struggle, and I'm not alone. I've often asked polished speakers if they ever got over stage fright, and they told me they still become apprehensive just before they get up. I'm the same way. But God has been faithful each week to remind me of His adequacy. As I get up to speak I quote to myself Isaiah 26:3-4: "Thou wilt keep him (me) in perfect peace whose mind is stayed on thee because he (I) trusteth in thee." And I remember 2 Corinthians 12:9: "My grace is sufficient for thee: for my strength is made perfect in weakness. Most gladly therefore will I rather glory in my infirmities, that the power of Christ may rest upon me."

I agree it's risky to stand in front of a group to teach. We may feel very vulnerable. Satan may use not only fear, but a whole set of circumstances to discourage us. You may be one of those people whose nervousness surfaces in insomnia or a weak stomach. Maybe your family was grouchy the night before the Bible study. Maybe just before you came you got an unpleasant phone call, opened a difficult letter, or ripped the hem out of your skirt. Maybe you had to rush out the door with a jar of jam spilled on your kitchen floor. You may think that God can never use you. There will be pressures, criticisms, testings and tears. You may feel so discouraged that you wonder if you should ever have tried to reach out to others.

But God promises to deliver us from all of it. Scores of times in His Word, God says, "Fear not." Remember, the only people who don't make mistakes or make themselves vulnerable to failure (or candidates for success) are the ones who don't do anything. They're the ones who have concluded that God couldn't possibly use them. Maybe they tried, made one mistake, and they quickly furled their sails, headed for shore and put the ship in dry dock. But the most precious teachers I know are those who didn't let failures discourage them. They remembered that the Lord upholds us with His hands (Psalm 37:24) and that "underneath are the everlasting arms" (Deuteronomy 33:27).

I may shake on the Rock, but He will never shake under me! There will be problems, but there will be rewards, too. Psalm 126:6 says:

> *He that goeth forth and weepeth, bearing precious seed, shall doubtless come again with rejoicing, bringing his sheaves with him.*

Those sheaves or reward will be spiritual children, changed lives, joyful women delighting in their God – and joy in your own soul that knows no bounds.

ALL
THINGS IN ORDER

God doesn't want a Bible study to be a one-woman circus. If you're a "loner" in wanting to start a Bible study, and feel that God would have you teach, pray for a friend who could take care of the mechanics of the study. We call this position the "coordinator." The Chris-Town study had a coordinator from the very beginning, not that we planned it that way, but as Jackie and I together began the studies, she naturally assumed the responsibilities. Over the years, other women took her place.

Both a teacher and a coordinator are important people in an organized Bible study. No study as it grows should be without a coordinating committee, too, to determine policy. And, responsibilities of the coordinator may have to be spread among various chairmen.

THE COORDINATING COMMITTEE

I think the "coordinating committee" that we established for decision-making at the Chris-Town study is completely in harmony with God's plans for checks and balances in spiritual leadership (see Acts 6).

The coordinating committee should be made up of three to five mature Christians who can be called on for particularly difficult matters. Through them God can govern the Bible study and keep it going in His directions. The members of the committee are usually chosen by the teacher and coordinator.

The committee should strive for unanimity on all decisions. The members should feel free to consult their husbands for opinions and ask advice of local pastors before reaching a decision. They should vote only after having prayed personally over the matter.

So far in the 18 years we have had a coordinating committee for the Chris-Town study there has never been a major disagreement in the whole group. We usually do not make a decision until we have unanimity. If there was a place of unresolved disagreement and all else failed, it might be best to let the decision rest with the teacher, although this should not happen often. If a decision cannot be made unanimously, it might be best to wait and bring up the subject again later.

Some of the matters which should come before the committee include:

1. **Bible study goals and doctrine.** These should be defined clearly and honored unless the Lord leads you to change. The Chris-Town committee has taken the stand that we are first of all a Bible study. Our purpose is to teach women the Word of God. All questions or suggestions must be evaluated in light of that basic principle.

We drew up a basic doctrinal statement which we use as our guide in choosing our teachers and leaders. This is implemented through a questionnaire each leader fills out (see appendix). Adherence to this basic statement helps maintain our unity. We also ask that women mention no churches or denominations during the studies. There will be areas of teaching where we may disagree, but we encourage women to disagree agreeably. (We have found there is little to disagree about when we have the Word of God open in front of us and we read the whole passage.)

Our only major area of disagreement has been over spiritual gifts. We believe that God is the One who divinely gifts persons through the Holy Spirit. We talk about the Giver, rather than emphasizing the gifts (1 Corinthians 13:1): "Though I speak with the tongues of men and of angels, and have not love, I am become as sounding brass, or a tinkling cymbal."

2. **Outside speakers.** Defining ourselves as a Bible study, we rarely have outside speakers. We decided that Christian Women's Clubs meet the needs of women to hear such speakers. Otherwise, we'd be deluged with recommendations for guest speakers and wouldn't get to our studies.

3. **Testimonies.** Instead of outside speakers, during the lesson time we often have one of the women in the study give a short testimony about what God is doing in her life. This will last from five to seven minutes. Women may also give testimonies in the small group studies (see chapter 6) but the length and content of these would be up to the discretion of the group leader.

4. **Special music.** The committee should decide how often to have special music and whether to have guest soloists. Special music can cause a problem because many will want to suggest their favorite musician. The

ORGANIZATIONAL CHART OF THE
CHRIS-TOWN WOMEN'S BIBLE STUDY

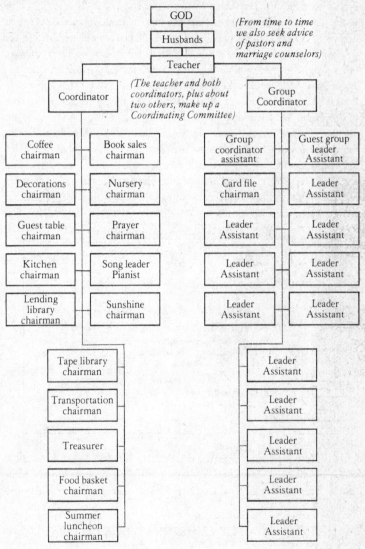

GOD

Husbands

Teacher

(From time to time we also seek advice of pastors and marriage counselors)

Coordinator

(The teacher and both coordinators, plus about two others, make up a Coordinating Committee)

Group Coordinator

Coffee chairman

Book sales chairman

Decorations chairman

Nursery chairman

Guest table chairman

Prayer chairman

Kitchen chairman

Song leader Pianist

Lending library chairman

Sunshine chairman

Group coordinator assistant

Guest group leader Assistant

Card file chairman

Leader Assistant

Leader Assistant

Leader Assistant

Leader Assistant

Leader Assistant

Leader Assistant

Leader Assistant

Tape library chairman

Transportation chairman

Treasurer

Food basket chairman

Summer luncheon chairman

Leader Assistant

Leader Assistant

Leader Assistant

Leader Assistant

Leader Assistant

Note: each chairman also has helpers

committee may want to limit special music to special occasions. A policy should be made — and kept.

5. Announcements and petitions. We keep our announcements to a minimum, using a bulletin board for miscellaneous notices. Outside activities, projects, speakers or missionary needs are usually worthy — but we voted years ago that we should promote very few of these or else the announcement time would take longer than the lesson. We do not allow petitions to be passed around. If we allowed one, we'd have to okay all — and the problems would mount.

We also do not advertise the Chris-Town study through the communications media. Our only advertisement is by life and word of mouth, and an occasional church bulletin announcement. From the beginning women have eagerly brought friends and relatives and the study continues to grow. We also have 2x3½-inch calling cards about the study which the women can give away.

Chris-Town

Women's Bible Study

"HAPPINESS IS - - - STUDYING GOD'S WORD"

- NON-DENOMINATIONAL
- NURSERY PROVIDED
- LUNCHEONS

THURSDAY, SEPT. THRU MAY, 9:15-11:30 A.M.
HELD AT **BETHANY BIBLE CHURCH**
6060 NORTH 7TH AVENUE

6. Time schedule, meeting place. The nuts-and-bolts of the Bible study — when and where to meet — should also be confirmed by the committee. The time schedule which Chris-Town found satisfactory is given in chapter 3.

THE COORDINATOR

I like to think of the Bible study coordinator as the staple in my stapler, gas in my car, sharpener for my pencil, stitch in my seam, shine on my silver and sugar in my tea. She can help me solve frustrating problems, find out what's lost, locate that overhead projector, find a blackboard, speak to the man whose power lawnmowing overpowers my lecture, rush

an injured babysitter (or child with mother) to the emergency room, repri-
mand a child the sitter can't handle, come up with an emergency supply of
diapers, make sure there are enough chairs, and run a lost-and-found for
potluck dishes. She can try to answer questions from 20 people at once, do
anything no one else wants to do, or forgot to do, and at the same time look
above the circumstances and know that this is where God wants her – and
love every minute of it.

God has designated some of His gifts to be "speaking" gifts and some
to be "helping" gifts (see chapter 4). Those with "speaking" gifts become
the teachers, but those with "helping" gifts are the best coordinators.
You'll be able to recognize a potential coordinator because she is:

1. *A growing Christian.* She will reflect Christ-like patience and
kindness, manifesting love to those around her. She need not be as
proficient in Scripture as the teacher but she should be walking in
obedience to God. Both the coordinator and the teacher will be watched by
the other women as examples of godly living.

2. *Helpful.* She should be the one who comes early and stays late, offering to help in various ways.

3. *Organized.* She should have an organized mind, be able to plan
ahead, and have some good ideas on how to make something better. She
will be the person who has — and uses — a notebook.

4. *Flexible.* She should communicate well with people, knowing when
to be as bendable as a shoot of bamboo, and when to be as firm as a
floodgate. She'll often become the buffer for problems.

5. *An encourager.* Besides a manager, she will be an encourager to the
teacher and other leaders. A coordinator need not start out as the teacher's
best friend, but the two will become close friends quickly as they work
together, sharing their burdens and joys. If there is any conflict between
the teacher and coordinator, the whole group will suffer. Therefore it is
important that they keep their communication lines open to each other. If
there are any hard feelings they should talk it out and pray about it. The
instruction is in Ephesians 4:30-32:

> *And grieve not the Holy Spirit of God, whereby ye are sealed
> into the day of redemption. Let all bitterness, and wrath, and
> anger, and clamor, and evil speaking, be put away from you, with
> all malice: and be ye kind one to another, tender-hearted, forgiv-
> ing one another, even as God for Christ's sake hath forgiven you.*

The success of a Bible study is at stake in the health of a relationship
between the teacher and her coordinator, and in their individual walks
with the Lord.

The Bible teacher, too, must encourage her coordinators and chairmen to get involved in either the first-hour study or a second-hour group. If their jobs are so demanding they feel they cannot take in the studies, get them extra helpers. It is easy for leaders to get "too busy" to participate — but we have seen negative results when they neglect the spiritual end of their Bible study involvement.

THE JOBS CHAIRMEN

The coordinator has general oversight for the chairmen of various responsibilities that a large Bible study involved. In turn, each chairman will have helpers, the number depending on her task and needs. At Chris-Town, we have women in charge of the pre-prayer time, treasury, nursery, coffee, guest table, kitchen, tape ministry, lending library, book sales, food baskets, summer luncheons, decorations, sunshine, transportation, plus a song leader and pianist. The duties of each will be explained later.

The chairmen should also comply with the doctrinal statement required of the teachers and coordinator. In essence, they are often in training for greater responsibilities. The chairmen should love the Lord and others, be enthusiastic, always look their best and have spirit-controlled temperaments, not easily upset. Like others in leadership, they will be watched for the quality of their walk with Christ, particularly by women who are not Christians.

The coordinator should meet with all the chairmen at the beginning of the year, giving them job descriptions and answering any questions they may have. During the year she should meet with each individually, to answer any questions or suggest solutions to problems in their areas.

If a chairman cannot come on a particular day, or must leave early, she should find a substitute from an approved list of helpers. This will prevent the responsibility from falling back on the coordinator.

Anyone who accepts a responsibility for the Bible study should regard it as an important responsibility and should not, for example, schedule doctor or dental appointments at the same time as Bible study.

Here are the duties of the various chairmen at Chris-Town:

1. PRAYER

A women's Bible study is a spiritual battlefront. Satan will do all he can to disrupt plans, confuse people and destroy the effectiveness of the study. But 1 John 5:14-15 assures us that we can confidently pray for those things which are according to God's will — and the defeat of Satan's distractions is certainly His will!

Therefore we have a prayer chairman arrive about half an hour before the Bible study to lead others who wish to pray on behalf of the study. They gather in a quiet room away from the lecture hall. All group leaders, of course, should pray at home for the study, too. But the time together on Thursday mornings should bring special attention to the various needs of the study.

They pray for the salvation of women and husbands. They pray for guests who may be frightened as they come. They ask God's touch for the song leader and that the music might set the right tone for the day. They ask God's anointing for the speaker so her message will have God's power and not be mere words. They pray for prepared hearts, so the Word will fall on good ground (Mark 4:14-20). They pray for group leaders, assistants and other helpers, for their responsibilities and that God's job may be seen in their hearts and on their faces.

The prayer chairman should, of course, be a woman of prayer — one who firmly believes in the exercise of this privilege and that, as God said through James, "Ye have not, because ye ask not" (James 4:2).

Every week women comment on how special our Bible study is. We know the secret. God is at work through prayer.

2. TREASURY

Unlike the other helping posts, this one requires no "helpers." The treasurer, however, does work closely with the coordinator. She is responsible for the study's financial transactions and for seeing that all bills are paid. She informs the coordinator of any shortage. We have found that in such cases the women dig deeper into their own purses to keep the study in the black.

If your group is bordering on the red side of the ledger, you may need to reevaluate your expenses. We found, for example, that we had to stop giving baby gifts because too many women were having babies and we couldn't handle the cost!

The treasurer pays for the:

— Babysitters
— Materials used for children's Bible class.
— Rent
— Office supplies (paper for printed lessons, transparencies, pens, stencils)
— Liability insurance, taken out in case of accident. In 18 years we had only two minor situations which required insurance, but we are glad we had it.

The treasurer should keep track of group finances not only on checkbook stubs but in a ledger which can be checked at a glance.

3. NURSERY

Children are important to mothers. A good nursery is vital to a good Bible study. Unless you have a nice, clean room and good babysitters, the young mothers will not come.

You will find that the Bible study will grow in proportion to its nursery facility. As the study grows, your nursery will also have to grow. We found that we had to expand into other rooms.

The woman who takes this responsibility should love children and work well with adults. The chairman could be one of your faithful Christian sitters.

The situation. Obtain the best nursery situation possible. Keep the nursery near the mothers, but avoid having it in the same house so mothers can concentrate on the lesson. Invite mothers to bring toys to equip the nursery. If there are not enough, the coordinator may have to buy toys but she will need to be reimbursed. You will need volunteers to wash the toys and sheets. Prepare two babysitting guides — one for what is expected of sitters, and the other to give mothers telling what is expected of them and their children.

The sitters. By all means, hire sitters. Never ask mothers to take turns sitting the children. There are two good reasons to hire women to watch the children. First, a mother should have one day a week out without having to babysit other people's children. Second, she would miss the Bible study and it would be hard for her to catch up.

We get names of sitters by calling churches in the area, asking for names of women who sit in their Sunday nurseries. We pray for Christian sitters but this is not always possible. The sitters are often older women who like to babysit to earn a little extra money. We pay them the current babysitting rate. We consider this a valid expense, because these sitters are helping us reach young women for Christ. We pay for the sitters from volunteer offerings. We do not require mothers to pay a certain amount. Sometimes the older women will put in extra to make up the difference. The treasurer should keep good records of who is paid and how much.

We also keep a roster of all available sitters in case of emergency. In addition, it is wise to keep attendance figures for the nursery, for future reference.

We seek out a Child Evangelism teacher for the two- through five-year-olds. If one is not available, pray for a woman who loves the Lord and children and wants to teach them. The children will love their special "Bible study" and want to come back — and of course this helps their mothers want to return, too. God has used little children's songs and words to soften their daddies' hearts. At Christmas time we usually have the children visit the mothers' study to show us what they have learned and to sing for us.

A word on discipline: sitters are not to spank or harm children physically or mentally. If they cannot handle the problem they are to come to the coordinator for assistance.

The significance. Nursery facilities may seem like a minor part of the Bible study, but they are more important than you think. The success of the study lodges in large part in freeing mothers of their motherly responsibilities long enough to concentrate on the Word of God. When you reach a mother for Christ, you really reach the whole family. She begins to love her husband and children more and becomes a better homemaker, excited and content to be God's woman in the home and in her community. In reality, we are reaching the world for Christ.

4. COFFEE TABLE

Hot coffee is a good ice melter, in more ways than one! I've heard many say it's easier to approach a stranger with a cup of coffee in your hand. The "regulars" drop their coins for coffee into a dish on the coffee table labeled "Donations." Newcomers get their coffee free.

The woman in charge of coffee not only sees that the beverage is perked and hot (iced tea is also provided), but that the table is decorated attractively.

5. GUEST TABLE

The guest table will be one of a newcomer's first impressions of the Bible study. Here she will be greeted and given a name tag. Here, too, will be replacement name tags for those who come regularly.

As with other helpers, those at the guest table consider prayer an important part of their preparation. They pray for the women who will be coming, for their sensitivity to various needs they may be encountering as greeters.

The guest table hostess and her helpers (she should have at least two in a large study) should be there at least half an hour to 45 minutes ahead of time to set up the table so it will be ready for the first women who come. The table should be located at the main entrance, large enough so it will not become too crowded when most people arrive.

The hostess should watch for first-time guests who may come early, waiting for the person who invited them.

The guest table helpers should find a greeting which is friendly but which does not require long answers. If they get too busy talking they may miss someone. They should be able to remember faces so that they do not have to ask, "Are you a first-timer?" This can be particularly ego-shattering to a woman who has been there several weeks.

Avoid leaving a guest alone unless she prefers it that way. Try to enlist "regulars" who will sit with guests who come along, and watch for the guest the following week, too. This will make them feel wanted. Remember, though, that some women prefer to sit alone, so don't push.

When they arrive, the guests should be given a special name tag (in the shape of a butterfly, flower, Bible, etc.) so the other women can easily identify them as newcomers and specially greet them. The "regulars" are asked to wear permanent name tags fastened with a small safety pin. There should be extra permanent tags at the guest table for women who forget or lose theirs. We've had women tell us: "My baby chewed it on the way home," "Mine went through the washer," "My dog ate it," or "It's in my other (purse, Bible, car, coat)."

All first-timers are also asked to fill out a card which looks like this:

```
┌─────────────────────────────────────────────────────────────┐
│ (Please Print)              Date _____ │
│                                                                │
│ ─────────────────────────────────────────────────────────────│
│ Last Name          First          Husband's Name              │
│ ─────────────────────────────────────────────────────────────│
│ Address            Zip Code            Phone No.              │
│ I am under 40 _____ 40 or over _____ │
│                                                                │
│ _____ I am a guest today and                            │
│                                                                │
│         I was invited by _____ │
│                                                                │
│ If needed, I would be willing to help                          │
│                                                                │
│   ☐ Typing                    ☐ Kitchen (on luncheon days)    │
│                                                                │
│   ☐ Book Sales or Lending Library  ☐ Hostess (on luncheon days)│
│                                                                │
│   ☐ Tapes                     ☐ Telephoning                   │
│                                                                │
│   ☐ Decorations               ☐ Door Greeter                  │
│                                                                │
│   ☐ Coffee                    ☐ Guest Table  ☐ Other Areas    │
└─────────────────────────────────────────────────────────────┘
```

6. KITCHEN

We have a potluck luncheon a particular Thursday of each month. Everyone brings a large dish of any food and 25¢ to defray expenses of coffee, paper plates and plastic tableware.

The kitchen chairman and her helpers may have to miss much of the first hour of study and all of the second to prepare for the luncheon. Tables must be set up, and food arranged. Later she will need volunteers to help with the cleanup.

The luncheons last from 11:30 to 1 p.m. The nursery is kept open and we pay the sitters for the extra time, of course.

7. TAPE MINISTRY

Several women are in charge of the various aspects of the tape ministry:

a. Taping the lesson and reproducing extras.

b. Supervising the tape library.

c. Mailing tapes requested out-of-town.

The tape library chairman and her helper each week make available a full variety of tapes for the women to check out. The women can request the tapes from a typed list of all those available. The chairman or her helper handle the checkout cards, which categorize each tape by author, subject, title and scripture. Tapes may be checked out before and after the Bible study, but not during.

The tapes are also sold (for price of blank tape plus postage) and mailed throughout the states. The current mailing list even includes a missionary in Africa.

For many women who have moved away from the Chris-Town study, the tapes are a welcome visitor. Typical of those is Cathy, who wrote:

"The tapes are an answer to prayer. Since we moved here I've felt very lost. Especially I missed the Bible study. There are only three churches in our new town, and none is compatible with how I believe. So, I haven't been attending church although I am listening to good Bible programs on radio and television. I've been telling women I met here about our Bible study in Arizona, and I shared the tapes I brought with me. I'm so glad you will now be mailing tapes so I can invite several over to listen to them with me. But even if no one comes, it will be a fantastic blessing to me to be able to share in my Bible study. I am so hungry for the Word. I can't describe how I feel. Please thank everyone concerned with your fantastic tape mailing service, for now I, too, can be a part of my beloved Bible study group again."

8. LENDING LIBRARY

Women are readers, and our lending library is popular. We insist that any books for loan or sale (book sales are described in the next section) be doctrinally sound. Thus we ask that the women in charge of these areas read and evaluate any book before it is put on the shelf.

The librarian, of course, should be a woman who enjoys reading. Familiarity with a wide variety of books will help her recommend titles to women with various needs.

Our checkout system is simple. For our information, we ask each woman to fill out a 3x5 card with her name, address and phone number.

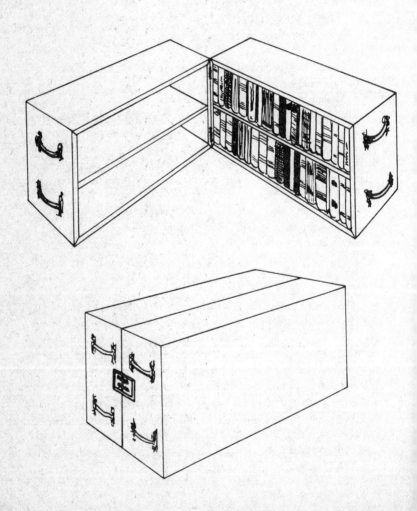

To check out a book (two-week limit) she needs only sign her name and the date to the check-out card in the book and give that to the librarian. The librarian calls women to remind them of any overdue books.

For obvious reasons, the lending library and book sales tables should not be opened until a librarian or helper are present. We close both book tables at 9:10 a.m. in order to give everyone an opportunity to participate in the singing. They open again after the Bible study, at 11:30 a.m.

Our book shelves for the lending library are portable, consisting of two hinged oblong boxes which one of the husbands constructed. Each box holds two shelves of books.

9. BOOK SALES

Books for sale are spread out on a table. They are sold at regular retail price, after being evaluated for doctrinal soundness. We obtain our books from a local Christian book store at a good discount. The book sales chairman keeps an account of all sales. At the end of the year all unsold books are returned to the store. Profits are put in the Bible study treasury and used for such needs as booklets explaining salvation or new books for the library, and other needs.

We have at least 200 books for sale, including children's books. Often women will stop at the sales table to tell how God used a particular book to bring a parent to Himself, or to save a friend's marriage.

10. FOOD BASKETS

Several times a year (not just at Thanksgiving and Christmas) we collect food for needy families. The food basket chairman, her husband and sons have made this their family ministry. At home they divide up the food, arrange the boxes and then make a special outing out of driving to recipients' homes in their 1931 Model A pickup.

"The families greet us with such appreciation," this chairman says. "Sometimes the kids can't wait to begin digging through the groceries. Sometimes we are invited in for a cup of coffee. Jesus said that it is more blessed to give than to receive. But no one could possibly be more blessed, nor receive more joy, than we do through sharing these boxes of food."

11. SUMMER LUNCHEONS

Summer vacation for the school children means a summer break for the regular Bible study, too. Otherwise, as large as our group is, we could never handle the enlarged babysitting load. For other reasons, too, we need a break. But in recent years we have seen a need for some sort of continuity and so now during the summer have monthly luncheons. These occasions meet the needs of many women for fellowship, encouragement, and teaching. Some may not yet be in a Bible-teaching church or their husbands may not want them to attend church. Without summer meetings, fellowship and encouragement would be severely restricted.

The summer luncheon chairman and her helpers choose a place to meet (a restaurant, or a church for a potluck), plan decorations (if any) and buy supplies (such as paper plates), and arrange for a speaker and/or Bible teacher, testimony and special music.

Each summer group should also decide whether to include a nursery service. At Chris-Town we have a summer nursery only for children of the helpers.

Each group, too, must determine which day to meet. We chose Thursdays, the same day as the regular Bible study. We prefer to have the study, music and testimony from 10 to 11:30 with the luncheon following. We find it is better to study in the morning than after lunch.

The women are encouraged to bring guests. Many women have received the Lord and gotten their start in Bible study through the summer luncheons.

12. DECORATIONS

One woman sees that there are attractive decorations for the coffee and guest tables each week, for the monthly luncheons and for any special occasion such as the evening couples' potlucks. We consider decorations important because they contribute to a warm, cheerful atmosphere and in general set the tone for the entire occasion. We once sold the centerpieces at each luncheon, but have found it easier and more economical to keep and reuse them. It is not necessary to have different decorations each year. From time to time new ideas can be introduced, as the Bible study budget allows.

The decorations chairman may want to work with a committee. Or, because distance may make it difficult for a committee to get together for a work time, she may prefer to work alone.

13. SUNSHINE

The sunshine chairman sends appropriate cards with a Bible verse for births, deaths and hospital stays. The cards go only to women in the study or their immediate families. Names come through group leaders.

The chairman buys cards by the box (they are less expensive that way) and chooses styles which include a Bible verse. She keeps the cards in a metal file box along with a card file on every card she sends. Funds for the cards and stamps come out of the Bible study treasury.

14. TRANSPORTATION

The transportation chairman matches those who need rides with those willing to give rides. We consider this an important function since we do not want to deprive anyone who has no transportation of the opportunity of hearing God's Word.

The chairman usually uses our Bible study address/phone directory to line up rides. Leaders help by inquiring in their groups if any need a ride or are willing to pick up others. A signup sheet to match riders and drivers could also be placed on a bulletin board, but we find it better to coordinate the rides through group leaders.

15. SONG LEADER

A singing time at the beginning of the Bible study helps prepare hearts and minds to be open to the Word of God. The song leader can use an overhead projector for lyrics or pass out song sheets. She is also responsible for having an accompanist each week. She closes the singing time with a short prayer and by announcing the day's program (testimony or special soloist, and teacher).

THE
JETHRO SOLUTION

Two major problems wormed their way into our Bible study group in those early years. First, the women differed dramatically in their familiarity with Scripture. Some had studied the Bible for years and wanted to pursue deeper studies. Some were such babes in the Word that they had trouble looking up references; their greatest need was a basic Bible study. Second, more women coming meant more counseling needed, and it seemed I was endlessly on the phone talking with women who needed personal help.

How could I teach and counsel all of the women? About the time that the dilemma reached a climax I was reading in Exodus 18. There Moses was overwhelmed by all the "counseling" he had to do. From morning to evening he sat as people filed by, presenting their problems for his solution.

Then his father-in-law Jethro came for a visit. Jethro just as much as said, "Moses, this is ridiculous. If you don't get some help pretty soon, you're going to be a basket case. Get some godly men to help you judge and counsel."

Jethro, who also trusted God, had a method (see Exodus 18:5-22). He suggested Moses pick out God-fearing men to rule over thousands, hundreds, fifties, and tens – "and let them judge the people at all seasons: and it shall be, that every great matter they shall bring unto thee, but every small matter they shall judge: so shall it be easier for thyself, and they shall share the burden with thee" (Exodus 18:22).

Here was my situation! And God's solution! In black and white! As I prayed about it, God showed me that He wanted me to share the teaching load by using mature, godly women to lead smaller discussion-study groups during a second hour of the Bible study. Throughout these groups, too, would be women who could be available for any counseling needs. Some counseling would still come my way, and we knew, too, that when we felt we could not help, we could refer these women to a pastor or professional counselor.

Addition of second-hour Bible study leaders, though, made some more administrative help necessary. It wasn't something that the coordinator should take on, too, with all she already had to do with the mechanics of running the study. Thus we appointed another "coordinator" whose responsibilities would be limited to running the second-hour format. Joyce, one of our first "group coordinators," was a school teacher who brought to the new concept good ideas in teacher training. When the time came that she had to give up her coordinating responsibilities, they shifted to Cherie, one of our group leaders whom God had especially prepared for the role through training in her church. As she used her expertise in Bible-teaching techniques to train our group study leaders, the Bible study as a whole was tremendously strengthened.

WHY HAVE SMALL GROUPS?

There is a big difference between hearing about the Bible and actually studying it. You may hear about the discovery of a fabulously rich gold mine in Rizmat and briefly remark, "Hmmmm, how interesting." But if you are the person in Rizmat biting the earth with your pickax, ecstatically watching gold nuggets spill out of the rock — well, that's an entirely different thing! Listening to teaching about the Word of God is good. But discovering Bible truths yourself and sharing them is like being on the human end of the pickax. Small groups fit in here, enabling people to learn more as they become personally involved in the learning process.

What can small groups do for a Bible study?

1. They enable women to learn at their own rates and to study topics they are interested in.

2. They help women learn to dig out spiritual truths through homework and memory verse assignments.

3. They encourage closer fellowship. The women usually sit in a circle and as they see each other's faces each week they learn to love and to care for each other.

4. They provide a training ground for leaders.

5. They provide women with needed opportunities to meet new friends. Each group is encouraged to have occasional luncheons to help the women get to know each other better.

WHAT SHOULD BE OFFERED?

The small groups should be tailored to meet women's needs.

The first division of needs would be between those who want a basic Bible study and those who want to study Scriptures more deeply. We found this basic diversity exists when your general study grows to 10 to 15 women. As your main group grows, you can add more study groups between the "'basics" and the "deeps." Groups studying the "basics" should be no larger than 12.

The Chris-Town Bible study grew to 30 second-hour groups geared to four levels of spiritual maturity. (This number was reduced when the study was divided to create another study in a new part of town.) What works for Chris-Town may not work for another group, but we explain our structure here in case it may help someone else.

GUEST GROUP — This is one of our most important groups. After the general Bible study hour, all first-timers are taken to our nicest room where they can relax in comfortable chairs and chat over coffee and cookies. We ask them to introduce themselves (they stood as a group during the first hour) and they have a short get-acquainted time. Then the group leaders give a no-pressure presentation of the plan of salvation. We use the Billy Graham booklet, "Peace With God." They can check a box in the booklet if they have made a decision for Christ that day or if they want to receive follow-up material.

The leader of the Guest Group gives a brief presentation about the Bible study, emphasizing that it is non-denominational and we do not mention churches by name. She also tells about the couples' evening Bible studies, the book and tape libraries, book sales, restroom and nursery and monthly luncheons. The newcomers are encouraged to enroll in a second-hour group geared to the their spiritual needs. During the last 15 minutes the small groups coordinator comes in to register them. When they return the second week, they are taken to the group they chose.

LEVEL 1 — BASIC STUDIES. This is for new Christians or non-Christians. New groups are started as needed during the year. We use the first books in the Campus Crusade or Navigators study series as well as other studies or lessons prepared by the leaders. Our classes are titled: "A New Life in Christ," "Life At Its Best," and "Getting to Know Jesus."

LEVEL 2 — LEARNING TO GROW. Our classes are: "The Holy Spirit and You" (Campus Crusade book), "How-to's of the Christian Life" (Crusade material), "Fellowship With Christ" (Navigators material), "Time Alone With God" (material developed by leader from

Psalms, on the daily devotional life), "Is Life Really Worth Living?" (study of John), "Abiding in God's Smile" (study of 1 Thessalonians), "Matthew: Behold Your King" (study helps from J. Vernon McGee on Matthew), "Happiness Is — Sharing Your Faith" (Crusade material).

LEVEL 3 — MEETING LIFE'S CHALLENGES. These are our specialty groups: "Two Peas in a Pod" (on marriage), "No Greater Joy?!?" (for mothers of preschool children), "Joy of Living in the Home" (study of Philippians as it relates to the home), "Problems in the Home" (for serious home problems: see chapter 7), "Being a Woman of God" (for young unmarried women under 25 years), "Tour of Woman's World" (study of women in the Bible), "40-Plus" (for women facing adjustments like the empty nest, in-laws, grandmothering, retirement, being a lover, death and living alone).

LEVEL 4 — DIGGING DEEPER INTO GOD'S WORD. These include: "Something Old, Something New" (Hebrews), "Strength for Struggles" (Joshua), "In the Beginning" (Genesis), "Pictures of Christ" (study of the tabernacle), "Voices of Twelve Hebrew Prophets" (minor prophets), and "Ten Basic Doctrines."

These subjects and the number of groups vary from year to year.

In addition to these we have also started a class for women who want to lose weight. Forty-five minutes before the general study they meet to "weigh-in," report their weight loss or gain, encourage and pray for each other. A nursery is provided for these "early-comers."

Each of the second-hour classes is based on the Bible. Any materials are only supplementary. We consider the Bible our study book. A review committee looks over any new material before it is used to make sure it is doctrinally sound.

We also try to avoid duplicating materials and studies during the couples' evening studies. For example, if we use a Navigator guide at the couples' studies, we generally do not use that same guide for the women's Bible studies.

Our enrollment procedure is as simple as possible. We have a two-semester Bible study year which parallels the school year. (When our numbers were smaller we continued all year around, but with our present number it would tremendously increase our babysitting load and we would not have the rooms for all the added children.) During the first three weeks of September we meet only in the large group. This is to give the women a chance to find out if they would like to continue in the Bible study and get involved in a group. The third week we hand out an information sheet on classes, explaining the content, naming the leader and assistant, and listing cost of materials (none over $3). The women are given a week to pray about the classes and name their first three choices and the following week during small-group hour they register. As each leader and her assistants note their enrollment has reached its limit (according to how many they have stated they can handle), they take the registered women to their classroom. The leader introduces the material and lets them know which books they should purchase at the book table (she previously ordered enough from the book chairman). She tells her goals for the class, assigns homework, and allows a short get-acquainted time before they are dismissed.

A woman who does not get her first choice registers for her second or third choice. An information table is maintained throughout the registration hour to handle any other problems.

After registration day, we make up a summary sheet of open classes to share in the Guest Group. They can enroll in these classes for the next four to five weeks. Of course, we start groups as needed throughout the year. A woman may begin coming to Bible study any time of the year, therefore, and find a second-hour class in which she would not be too far behind. We also have had special studies for the final four or five weeks of the semester to accommodate latecomers. Most of all, we try to be flexible.

Women may come for the first-hour study only, if they desire. Of course, they balance their study of the Bible and enjoy more fellowship through the second-hour small group, and so we encourage them to stay the whole morning.

WHO SHOULD LEAD THE STUDIES?

We are amazed to see how God sends us Bible study leaders. When the study was small, it was easier to know the women and determine who was spiritually maturing and qualified as a teacher. Growth has complicated this selection, but God has used these guidelines to help us select just the right women:

1. *Ask leaders for prospects.* In each class, particularly in the "deeper" studies, certain women will stand out as potential leaders. Their names are given to the group coordinator, who in turn contacts these women and tells them that they have been recommended to serve as an assistant.

2. *Have the prospective assistant fill out a doctrinal questionnnaire.* Our questionnaire is four pages long and requires a woman to explain her beliefs in her own words and with Scripture. We allow her several weeks to fill it out and let her use any helps she wants. We explain that this is not a "test" but just a way for us to make sure we agree on doctrine. (See appen-

dix for example questionnaire.) We may differ on minor points, but if we have unity on the basics, then there is greater harmony in the entire Bible study. Most of the women have thanked us for this in-depth questionnaire as it helped them to solidify their beliefs with Scripture. Each is encouraged to make a photocopy of her study for future reference. The questionnaires are kept on file.

3. *Have the assistant write her personal testimony.* This should be a one- to two-page account of how she came to know Christ and what God has been, and is doing, in her life.

4. *Involve the assistant in leadership training.* Have her attend the monthly leadership meetings. Try to place her in the class of her choice. When classes change, encourage her to become an assistant under another teacher so she can benefit from learning from another. At the end of each semester, each leader will evaluate the assistant's helpfulness, dependability and readiness to lead independently. If the assistant feels she is not ready to teach or the leader feels the assistant could benefit from more experience, she is encouraged to serve again as an assistant. With few exceptions, assistants grow into leaders.

5. *Choose a leader for her attitudes and interests.* A group will take on the attitude of its leader, so choose leaders who demonstrate Christ-like attitudes. Place a leader in her area of interest. If she likes to work with new believers, place her in Level 1. Or if she is interested in teaching about the home, or studying Scripture in depth, place her in charge of that type of class.

The leader chooses study materials or personally develops lessons which must be approved by the materials review committee before they are taught. The group coordinator may make suggestions if a leader is unsure what to teach, but usually the coordinator asks the leader what God has been teaching her lately through His Word. This is her clue to what she might teach if she has no ideas otherwise. A leader teaches best where she has walked.

The responsibilities of a *leader* are:
1. To plan, prepare and pray for her group.
2. To attend all leadership meetings.
3. To train her assistant, letting her know what she expects of her.
4. To let the assistant lead the class occasionally when the assistant is ready for that responsibility.
5. To pray with the assistant for the women in her class.
6. To dress modestly (we say, "Look nice. Smell nice." Pantsuits are permissible).

7. To contact absentees in her class.

The responsibilities of an *assistant* are:

1. To support her leader.
2. To be dependable, calling the leader if she cannot attend.
3. To help make phone calls.
4. To keep attendance records.
5. To always do the homework and assigned memory work.
6. To help the leader in any way needed.
7. To pray regularly for the women in the group.
8. To attend leadership meetings.

The assistant should not monopolize a class, but join in like the rest of the group during discussion. She should lead the group in the absence of the leader.

HOW CAN GROUPS BE LED?

A small Bible study group should be:

• *Person-centered*
• *Bible-based in teaching*
• *Informal in learning*
• *Life-focused in understanding*

Striving for these qualities will help prevent it from becoming a place where people talk about their problems or pool their ignorance. Small groups are spiritual laboratories, where women methodically but earnestly prove the trustworthiness of God's Word and its application to their lives. They are search maps, not sitting rooms.

PERSON-CENTERED. We adapt a phrase from 1 Corinthians 13: "Though I have the gift of teaching and do not have love for the ones I teach, my teaching is empty." A leader can make her group people-centered by:

—Accepting people as they are.

—Being sensitive to individual needs.

—Being a good listener. Eye-to-eye contact says, "You are important to me." Do not be thinking about what you are going to say next.

—Calling each person by her first name at least once during the session.

—Refusing to "put down" a person for a wrong answer or for disagreeing.

—Affirming the group, letting them know you value them and bringing out their strengths.

—Sharing yourself. Don't wear a mask. Let them know that you feel, love and hurt. The leader should foster the attitude that this is *our* group.

BIBLE-BASED IN TEACHING. The Bible is our focus. The Holy Spirit is our Teacher. Psalm 19:7-8 tells what the Word can do for us:

> The law of the Lord is perfect, converting the soul: The testimony of the Lord is sure, making wise the simple. The statutes of the Lord are right, rejoicing the heart: the commandment of the Lord is pure, enlightening the eyes.

INFORMAL IN LEARNING. "Informal" does not mean "unplanned" but the leader has a lesson plan and knows how to carry it out. She has tailored it to her time slot and yet can change it according to needs. She never reads her lesson verbatim to the group. She is prepared, but not rigid.

We can learn a lot from the Master Teacher, Jesus. Much of His teaching was informal. The Gospels record some of His methods, for example:

—Object lessons to clarify: patches and wineskins (Matthew 9:16-17)

—Storytelling and illustrations: parable of the sower (Matthew 13:3-9)

—Visual aids: a little child (Matthew 18:2-3) and a penny (Matthew 22:17-21)

—Questions: Peter (Matthew 16:13-17) and the young lawyer (Luke 10:25-37)

Jesus helped people to think for themselves! Consider using some of His methods and others as you plan each lesson and seek ways to help the women discover truths for themselves. Some methods useful in encouraging group participation include:

1. Brainstorming

The teacher gives the class a word or topic. During a specified time limit, class members offer as many related ideas or solutions as possible, not waiting to be called on. These ideas are written on a chalkboard or overhead without comment. For example, to the teacher's word "believe" a class might respond with such terms as "rely," "depend" or "trust," and so on. After the "story," the class evaluates and discusses the ideas. This discussion technique loosens up a group, helps involve shy people, channels thinking and promotes new ideas. No one is intimidated, because there is no "right" or "wrong" answer.

2. Buzz groups

The teacher divides the class into small "buzz" groups of three to six persons each. (Small classes can work in two's.) Simultaneously, during a specified length of time, they discuss an assigned topic or try to solve a problem. When the entire class reconvenes a representative of the "buzz group" reports their findings or conclusions. This method helps maximize participation and interaction because many people feel freer to speak in small groups.

3. Class discussion

The teacher asks the class a question which has more than one acceptable answer. Class members interact with each other as well as with the teacher. The teacher keeps the discussion from straying, asks leading questions as necessary, and summarizes the discussion at the end. This method helps class members observe interaction techniques but may be weakened by people who dominate a discussion.

4. Study groups

The students have their Bibles open and the teacher asks questions to help them learn what the passage they are studying says. The class is encouraged to share insights about the passage's interpretation, principles and application. The teacher summarizes findings. This method helps class members learn to study the Bible individually and increases participation and involvement.

5. Listening groups

The teacher appoints teams to listen for certain truths or thoughts as someone reads a Scripture passage or discusses a subject. For example, the teacher may divide the group in half and then say, "As I read these verses, half of you tell us why Christ is 'in me,' and the other half tell us why I am 'in Christ.'" This technique increases alertness.

6. Question/answer interchange

The teacher asks questions to direct class discussion, perhaps starting with a few fact questions to lay a foundation (these often begin with "who," "when" or "where" and usually have only one answer) before moving into the thought questions (which usually begin with "why," "how" or "in what way"). The thought questions require a person to choose between two or more answers, interpret, make distinctions, prove motives or make application. For example, a teacher may ask, "In what ways was. . ." or "How would Jesus have reacted?" Using questions is a good way to review without being boring. Questions also help a teacher evaluate what is being learned, and can bring a wandering discussion back on the track.

7. In-depth Bible encounter

The teacher asks class members to individually write a Bible verse or passage in their own words, to help tell what that passage means. Class members also write out answers to the questions, "How does this apply to my life?" or, "If I took this passage seriously, what would I have to do?" The answers can be shared with the whole group or in sub-groups. This method helps class members learn to study the Bible independently.

Often in a group study, emotions and feelings come into the discussion. It becomes easy to say, "I don't see how it is possible for a loving God to do such a thing," or, "That is out-of-date . . . after all, this is the 20th Century." When this type of response surfaces the leader must politely but firmly bring the class back to the "standard" by saying, "What does the Bible, our sole authority, say?" This response will keep the study true to the Word and free from conjecture and error.

LIFE-FOCUSED IN UNDERSTANDING. It is insufficient to expose a person to Bible truth. It is not enough to lead an individual to understanding and appreciating the meaning of a Bible truth. Real learning takes place when the person integrates the truth into his lifestyle. Bible truths come alive when they meet an important life need. Therefore, the ultimate goal of all Bible study is application.

Following is a sample plan for a 55-minute to one-hour class.

1. Create learning readiness (3-10 minutes). This introductory step directs the students' thinking into the area of study and sparks their interest in the lesson. It can be accomplished various ways: brainstorming a word, making a debatable statement and asking for feedback, using visuals, asking launching questions, etc.
2. Bible study content (30 minutes). Don't lecture. Divide into buzz groups; try depth Bible encounter or questions and answers.
3. Personal application (15 minutes). Use any of the methods. Ask questions like, "What does this mean to you personally?", or, "If you took

this passage seriously, what changes would come into your life?" Action assignments can also be made.

4. Encourage further study (4 to 10 minutes). You are your best advertisement. Motivate your group to study for the next session. Assign homework, memory work and/or an action assignment. This is best done orally or written on the blackboard so they must also write the assignment down. This will help them start thinking immediately about the assignment. Pre-printed homework sheets tend to be forgotten for six days unless a teacher stirs interest in the contents.

HOW CAN A TEACHER MEET TEACHING PROBLEMS?

A teacher can expect problems, but she must not expect to be defeated by them. Problems will be minimized if she announces guidelines at the first class session. She may ask the women to agree or covenant together to:

1. Begin and end on time.

2. Be faithful in attendance.

3. Do homework. Remind them that they will get out of a class only what they put into it. Remember, however, that some women with babies or other heavy responsibilities will find it difficult to keep up the studies. Make them feel welcome and loved. In time they'll be able to study.

4. Participate. A teacher might comment, "Feel that you are a part of the group. What you have to share is important even if you are a beginner."

5. Refrain from dominating discussion so all can share.

6. Be understanding. The teacher may remark, "I believe each person is a separate and unique individual. Be sure to recognize that the needs, reactions and comments of others may be different from yours."

7. Don't mention churches.

SPECIFIC PROBLEMS

Specific problems a teacher may encounter include:

— *The talking machine.* If a woman dominates a discussion, try calling for contributions from others. Ask, "What do you others think?" Sometimes it is necessary to talk with the "talker" privately, explaining the necessity of group participation. Perhaps you can enlist her help in drawing out the quiet ones.

— *Vagrancy of the vocal chords.* To get a wandering discussion back on track, try a verbal recognition of the situation: "This is interesting, but let's get back to the topic." A thought-provoking question might also be used to draw their interest back to the subject.

— *"Dumb" questions.* All of us have had questions that we feel "dumb" asking. Tell the women no question is "dumb" but that the last day of the study will be called "Dumb Question Day." Any question *off the subject* they should write down and turn in to the leader for discussion and answer on that day. Have refreshments and make it a fun day.

— *Red-check answers.* Never flatly contradict a person who gives a wrong answer. Direct the same answer back to the group, saying, "That's interesting. What do others think?", or, "Has anyone some Scripture which may help us?" If the group never clarifies the answer, you may need to clarify it with Scripture. Or, when you summarize at the end make sure a wrong answer is corrected.

— *The problems problem.* If a woman repeatedly brings up her "problem," ask her to phone you and have lunch with you to talk it over. Don't let the entire group suffer for her woes. If her problem consumes every conversation, you might want to suggest that she attend the "Problems in the Home" group, or see one of the group counselors.

— *Lumps on logs.* Don't become anxious if a response is silence. Give people time to think and answer. Be an enthusiastic leader and people will respond enthusiastically. Develop good thought questions. People may prefer to write down their answers and then read them to the class. Or, you may want to divide the group into sub-groups until the women get used to sharing.

— *Shorts in your computer.* If you don't know the answer, say, "I don't know the answer." Don't fake it. But then, also add, "I'll find out," or have someone else research the answer. Many times someone in the group will know the answer. The leader recognizes she is a learner, too.

— *Tyranny of the urgent.* Don't become bogged down with details nor chase rabbits. Define your goal and keep with it. Keep your assignments clear and avoid assigning more than you can cover.

WHAT IF A LEADER BECOMES DISCOURGED?

The Bible gives leaders some truths to grab on to. Psalm 32:8 says, "I will instruct thee and teach thee in the way which thou shalt go: I will guide thee with mine eye." What a promise! He's going to instruct us, teach us and guide us!

And what if we feel insufficient, incapable, unable? 2 Corinthians 3:5 says, "Not that we are sufficient of ourselves to think any thing as of ourselves; but our sufficiency is of God." We can't stop at acknowledging our insufficiency. We must go on to acknowledge the absolute adequacy and sufficiency of God to meet any test, overcome any problem and win any battle. Philippians 2:13 says, "For it is God which worketh in you both to will and to do of his good pleasure." What more do we need?

Of utmost importance to leaders is their personal relationship and fellowship with the Lord Jesus Christ. If we starve ourselves spiritually, how can we feed others?

Three traps yawn at the feet of every leader:

1. *Comparison.* Comparing yourself with others is denying that God has a special place for you. 2 Corinthians 10:12 says, "For we dare not make ourselves of the number, or compare ourselves with some that commend themselves: but they, measuring themselves by themselves, and comparing themselves among themselves, are not wise." Your teaching must be unique and distinct from other teachers.

2. *Discouragement.* Refuse to look only at omissions and problems when you evaluate your teaching. Look also at what went right. Learn from the positive as well as the negative.

3. *Giving up.* Don't throw in the towel. Ecclesiastes 7:8 gives wise advice: "Better is the end of a thing than the beginning." When you have prayed about a responsibility and *know* it was God's will, return to that point and continue. In due time you will prosper. Just say to the Lord, "I'll be faithful to continue what you have led me to do. I'll not trust my roller-coaster *feelings* — but the *fact* that You said, 'Teach this group.' "

HOW SHOULD LEADERS BE TRAINED?

We hold leadership meetings monthly except during the summer. If your meetings are well-planned, your leaders will come. Some meetings should be for all leaders, assistants and helpers and some will be limited to leaders and their assistants. Plan to have several potlucks to help the women become acquainted. Provide a nursery.

The leadership meeting should consist of prayer, leadership training, encouragement, business, solving necessary problems, sharing of blessings, fellowship and Bible study. The same guidelines for small groups, such as starting on time, apply, too.

The meetings should be planned and directed by the group coordinator.

Here is a sample leadership meeting schedule:

9:30-9:45   Announcements by coordinator, group coordinator and/or lecture-teacher

9:45-10:30   Leadership training. We may have the group coordinator or another leader share methods and ideas on how to lead a group effectively. Whenever possible, put these methods into action in the leadership meeting.

10:30-11:10   In-depth Bible study in areas which will help your leaders strengthen weak areas and grow. Any capable person can lead this part.

11:10-11:30   Prayer time for needs of the Bible study. Divide into groups of four, or have leader and assistant pray together, or pray with someone you do not know well. Use variety.

We also sometimes invite women who are starting a new Bible study to participate in our leadership training meetings. This helps them without creating extra "advice" meetings for the Bible study teacher and coordinators.

Growth of your Bible study will make leadership meetings imperative for maintaining unity of goals and spirit. The encouragement and idea pool they provide are vital. The teacher training will strengthen and replenish your leadership.

HOW CAN THE STUDIES BE EVALUATED?

At the end of each year we ask the women to fill out an evaluation sheet. This not only helps us improve our Bible study, but a tear-off section at the bottom leads us to the helpers we will need in various areas for the next year.

We have changed the questionnaire yearly, but the one in the appendix of this book is typical.

CALMING
TROUBLED WATERS

PART I – WHO MAY COUNSEL?

Carlotta, one of my assistants, shook her head slowly as she told me about a woman in the home problems class.

"I just hope she goes to the counselor I recommended," she said. My mind clicked. I'd heard her say this before and I wondered if she considered herself incapable of helping these women.

"Carlotta, did you open the Scripture to her?" I ventured. "Did you show her what God's Word says about this particular problem?"

There was silence, then slowly and softly she said, "This area of giving out God's Word is one in which I need to grow. I know it. I must begin memorizing more Scripture. I realize it's what God's Word has to say that changes lives — not what I have to say."

I was reminded of myself in Carlotta. Twenty years before, when I told Louise, a close Christian friend, that I wanted to be a teacher and counselor for God, this wise woman responded:

"Then set about to learn God's Word, Naomi. Study, read and memorize it. It's work, but it's worth it."

At times we must recommend that women see a professional counselor. But I question whether everyone with a personal, spiritual or marital problem needs to see a professional. Not all can afford such help. And, I hasten to add, none can afford the "non-help" that often comes over the back fence, at the beauty shop, from parents and at times from trained counselors who do not parallel their counsel with the teachings of the Word of God.

This chapter is not intended to be a complete study on counseling — but it is written to assist those who seek to help others.

Since the day I became a Christian I have watched God setting people free to become all they want to be and all he meant them to be. I am convinced that the essential element in all of that is *love* — God's love, the liberating love. People also need *truth* — God's truth, given in love. Jesus said, "I am the way, the truth, and the life: no man cometh unto the Father, but by me" (John 14:6). He also said, "I am come that they might have life, and that they might have it more abundantly" (John 10:10). He wants us to live that abundant life through the power of the Holy Spirit (Galatians 5:16).

THE MESSAGE PEOPLE NEED

God's love for us is so great that He allowed His only Son, Jesus Christ, to die on a cruel Roman death device, the cross, as our substitute (1 Peter 3:18). Each one of us rightly should have hung there as the proper punishment for our sins against God. But He appointed Christ to take on Himself the sins of the entire world. Because of what Christ did, God holds no thoughts of rejection against us — only love and forgiveness. This is the message that people need — that He offers us His salvation, as a free gift, just for the taking (John 1:12, Revelation 3:20). Who can tell them this magnificent truth? You can! I can! If we have experienced this love and forgiveness, and know the joy of living the abundant life, we can share this with others. 2 Corinthians 5:19-21 tells us we *must* share these truths with others, because He has committed to us – His ambassadors — the ministry of reconciliation.

All people need love and understanding. They need salvation through Jesus Christ. They need to hear the truth of God's Word, given in love. They need to know how to live the abundant life, through daily obedience and confession to our Lord. They need to know God's plan for the Christian home, and for the wife of the non-Christian. Many — in fact, most — do not know these truths. Many are floundering, staggering through life as they seek and search for happiness but do not know where to look. We know it is only found in Christ. We know the answer.

FACING PROBLEMS

How can we keep still? Why do we keep still? Could it be because we believe that only the pastor and trained counselors can share the "Good News"? It's easy to feel this way when someone comes to you with a terrible problem. I remember well the morning after Bible study a woman came to me with tears racing down her face. As we found a quiet place to talk, she sobbed, "It's my father-in-law. I really hate him."

My first thought was to send her to her pastor. But just as quickly as that thought came, God spoke to my heart about trusting Him to lead me to help her.

"Can you forgive your father-in-law?" I asked quietly.

"Oh, no. I can't. No, never."

"Do you want to?"

"Oh, yes!"

"Do you know that God loves him?"

Her eyes flared. "Oh, no, He can't love him. He is too great a sinner!" she stormed.

"But, honey," I said, "Christ died for sinners and He died for him, too."

We opened the Bible and talked more about how God loves the sinner but hates the sin. She confessed her unloving spirit to the Lord and the peace of God flooded her heart as we prayed together before she left. God had set her free from the hate. The situation did not change, but a new love for her father-in-law was made possible that day. God has given her and her husband special grace in a very difficult situation. They are trusting God for his salvation. How thankful I am that He wants to use each of His children to lift another's burden!

You may ask, "What about all the wrong counsel being given?" We cannot control what other people say. But we should find out what God says on any given subject and be prepared to share it. I Peter 3:15 says: "But sanctify the Lord God in your hearts: and be ready always to give an answer to every man that asketh you a reason of the hope that is in you, with meekness and fear."

Through the women's Bible study we see lives and homes being changed from week to week. We see God use His Word to set people free from sin, guilt, depression and loneliness. We witness transformations in marriages as women hear — sometimes for the first time — that God loves them and their families, and has their best interests at heart. Nearly every week someone tells us she recently accepted the Lord because of the Bible study.

The same God who transforms lives through salvation and obedience to His Word is also the One who gives discernment and wisdom in counseling. He will teach us how to listen, how to sense the basic problems, and how to offer direction. God does not want us to merely listen. Proverbs 11:14 says, "Where no counsel is, the people fall." I have to disagree with those who say all people need is a listening ear. I know women who would call up friend after friend and tell them the same sad story over and over, like a needle caught in the groove of a record. That does them no good, and likewise does their patient friends no good. Usually, it worsens the problem as repetition deepens the hurt.

As I listen, I ask God for discernment before I speak. Is she a Christian? Is she bitter, resentful, angry? I watch for phrases like, "He says I never," or, "He says I always." These are clues to basic family problems. If it is a relationship problem I let a woman talk long enough for me to sense several things she might be doing to aggravate the problem. Then I stop her and discuss these areas with her.

At first in marriage problems a woman will usually say that her husband's remarks or complaints are untrue. I try to get her to see that it is more important at this time to find out why *he* thinks they are true. Then she usually will concede that there is an element of truth in what he says. This is the first step toward solving the problem. Then it is important to show her from God's Word how she can and must forgive her husband, and begin to move in a positive way toward him.

Deep inside, she usually knows what God's attitude is about her behavior and relationship to her husband. But she needs to be reminded of it and have it verified in God's Word. You as the counselor need to show her God's love and concern for her by yourself being loving and concerned. Ask God to help you not make her feel guilty or condemned. Tell her that *you* fail and that God forgives you. Show her 1 John 1:9 ("If we confess our sins, he is faithful and just to forgive us our sins, and to cleanse us from all unrighteousness") to assure her of God's forgiveness and love. If you speak the truth in love, she will respond in love. Very few women have refused to listen to God's solutions. And very few have not wanted to do God's will when the truth was presented in love. Of course, I know it's not me. It's the Holy Spirit using the Word and fitting it to their needs.

For several years I have limited my counseling to women who are in the Bible study or already Christians. I don't have enough time to deal with others, and I have also found that most women who are not in the Word are not really asking for Christian counseling. They only want us to agree with the world's philosophy and their hearts are not ready for what the Word of God would tell them. You may find you do well in counseling them. If so, that's great, and God bless you. But for me, it hasn't worked.

When God commanded the older women to be "in behavior as becometh holiness, not false accusers, not given to much wine," He also told them to teach the younger women:

> . . . to be sane and sober-minded – temperate, disciplined — and

to love their husbands and their children; to be self-controlled,
chaste, homemakers, good-natured (kind-hearted), adapting and
subordinating themselves to their husbands, that the word of
God may not be exposed to reproach — blasphemed or dis-
credited. (Titus 2:4-5, Amplified)

The Word of God is clear. Women are to teach other women. And
God has specifically designated the older women to be the ones to counsel
the younger women. (By no means, however, does this mean that the
younger, godly women cannot share what God has taught them.) He tells
us what we are to teach, and He tells us why: *"that the Word of God be*
not blasphemed." God's name is being shamed in many homes because
Christians are ignorant of God's plan for the home. I believe homes today
are in trouble because the older women have not been teaching the younger
women, according to God's plan. The job instead, has shifted to those
whose advice departs from the Word. I believe there is a mighty army of
older, godly women today who could be used to turn the tide of divorce
and immorality. And you might even be a member of that now-silent
army. If you love God and are obedient to His Word, then ask Him to
bring into your life a younger woman you could counsel. If He blesses your
counseling on this one-to-one basis, He will send others your way. In this
way, God's blessings will spread out in an ever-widening circle.

Trust God to teach you what to say. Isaiah said, "The Lord God hath
given me the tongue of the learned, that I should know how to speak a
word in season to him that is weary" (Isaiah 50:4). God wants us to share
His truths and *His* solutions. He wants us to help women look at themselves and how elements of disobedience in their lives might be contributing to their problems. It is usually hard for a woman to admit that
she is part of the problem. One husband aptly said, "Women have halos
which have slipped. They cover their eyes so that they cannot see what they
are doing wrong." The Holy Spirit through the Word of God is the only
One who can convict us of our sin. Hebrews 4:12 says that "the word of
God is quick, and powerful, and sharper than any two-edged sword, piercing even to the dividing asunder of soul and spirit, and of the joints and
marrow, and is a discerner of the thoughts and intents of the heart."

A woman who lets the Word of God expose her sin and weaknesses,
and who seeks to remedy the situation with God's solutions, may find her
problem will not change, but her reaction to the problem will. God has
comforted her with the truth that He "will never leave thee, nor forsake
thee" (Hebrews 13:5). She will begin to "trust in the Lord with all (her)
heart; and lean not unto (her) own understanding. In all (her) ways

acknowledge him, and he shall direct (her) paths" (Proverbs 3:5-6).

This leads us to an important concept in Christian counseling. We must make sure the women understand that they are not to do these "things" in order that their husbands will change, but rather that the Lord would be glorified. There may be a change in their husbands or their situation as a result. But the motives behind all their actions should instead be to please God!

> *And whatsoever ye do in word, or deed, do all in the name of the Lord Jesus, giving thanks to God and the Father by him . . . And whatsoever ye do, do it heartily, as to the Lord, and not unto men. (Colossians 3:17, 23)*

It is possible that a husband may never change completely, but God can give each woman a sweet spirit in the midst of a very trying situation. I have seen husbands begin to change because their wives were also changing, and both for the better.

God never promised lives without problems. The book of 1 Peter was given to tell us *why* we suffer!

> *In this you greatly rejoice, even though now for a little while, if necessary, you have been distressed by various trials, that the proof of your faith, being more precious than gold which is perishable, even though tested by fire, may be found to result in praise and glory and honor at the revelation of Jesus Christ. (1 Peter 1:6 -7 NASB)*

God uses troubles to perfect His children, to mature us. We grow the most in the hard places. Often when we recall a favorite verse of Scripture it is linked to a particular problem in our lives when God used His Word, through it sharing His spiritual "secrets" (Psalm 25:14).

Some of the leaders in the Chris-Town study have unsaved husbands. But God is loving these husbands through their wives, and we believe they will come to know the Lord. We believe that household salvation is God's plan for the family. God saved Noah and all his family, and Rahab and her family. Paul told the Philippian jailer, "Believe on the Lord Jesus Christ, and thou shalt be saved, and thy house" (Acts 16:31). The same was said in Joppa (Acts 11:14) and experienced in Corinth (Acts 18:8). 1 Corinthians 7:13-14 says that a believing wife who stays with her unsaved husband sanctifies her husband and their children: "else were your children unclean, but now they are holy." Psalm 103:17 says God's mercies are "from everlasting to everlasting upon them that fear him, and his righteousness unto children's children." We have His position in the Word. *But we cannot put a time limit on the "when."*

Margaret, a close friend, prayed for her husband for 25 years before he received Jesus. She remained faithful and sweet through the good and bad times, believing confidently that he would be saved. The two years he lived after his salvation he was a tremendous testimony. She now says, "It was worth it all."

Many today opt for divorce, saying "God doesn't want me to be unhappy." Usually they add, "After I am divorced I will look for a Christian man so I can be happy." But it is God's will for us to work at the marriage we have — because it can get better — rather than face the same old problems (plus some) with a new partner. Women married to unsaved or non-growing husbands must be willing to wait upon the Lord. Psalm 27:14 says, "Wait on the Lord: be of good courage, and he shall strengthen thine heart: wait, I say, on the Lord." They must turn their expectations over to Him (Psalm 62:5). If they do, God will honor their faith and use their obedient lives to bring their husbands to Christ and to a close walk with God. (For a fuller discussion on this, see Dr. Paul Meier's article, "Divorce Is Never Necessary," in the appendix.)

Another important truth that counselors should share with their women is that there will be ups and downs. Almost always after they have made a step of faith, and begun to love their husbands with Christ's love, there will be times of failure. The women should know that this is when Satan wants to twist a believer into defeat. But if they are forewarned about times of discouragement, they will be better able to go to the Lord and ask for His mercy and grace (Hebrews 4:16).

Counselors should help the women to be realistic, setting goals that can be achieved. They should show them, by life and by the Word, how each can become a virtuous woman like the one described in Proverbs 31.

UNGODLY ADVICE

There is a vast difference between the advice shared in Christian counseling and that which the world offers. Psalm 1:1 warns us to walk "not in the counsel of the ungodly." Yet many women *do* follow the thought patterns of the ungodly when they are unprepared with Scripture's solutions to their problems.

The world's ungodly advice usually takes the form of comments like this:

1. "Leave your husband. He will never change."
2. "Kick your husband out of the house."
3. "You are right. He is wrong."
4. "Go home to your folks." Or, "Come home to us. You know you always have a place to come."

5. "Get a job and live as you want."
6. "You be the head of the home. He's doing a lousy job."
7. "If you don't divorce him, you'll lose everything. You'd better get a lawyer so you can be sure you are taken care of."
8. "It would be better for your children to have no daddy than the one they have."
9. "Walk out of the room when you are having a disagreement; you don't have to take that. Better yet, walk out of the house. That will show him!"
10. "If he has another woman, withhold your love from him, or leave him. That will make him suffer, too. You'll never be able to forgive him anyway."

Remember the statements above are ungodly advice. Bad advice. But this is the advice many women get from friends, neighbors, parents, co-workers and even some Christians. Those who know God's Word, however, know that this is not God's advice.

I have been asked if I ever counsel anyone to leave or divorce her husband. I must say I never have. This may surprise you since you might expect an occasional exception. My answer is that God is the God of the impossible. If you want a blessing, allow Him to change your attitudes and watch Him work. I have seen Him change impossible situations because the wife let God change her attitude. A wife should be willing to pray, as David did in Psalm 139:23-24, "Search me, O God, and know my heart: try me, and know my thoughts: And see if there be any wicked way in me, and lead me in the way everlasting."

We must give our counselees *hope*. Nothing is hopeless. God loves these women and their spouses, and He loves their homes. He wants their homes to be a testimony for Him (Titus 2:5). And He wants to help them. When women are distressed or depressed I show them Romans 15:13:

Now the God of hope fill you with all joy and peace in believing, that ye may abound in hope, through the power of the Holy Ghost.

Besides hope, they must recognize that a change in the situation may involve a change in themselves — in their attitudes. God wants them to be "casting down imaginations, and every high thing that exalteth itself against the knowledge of God, and bringing into captivity every thought to the obedience of Christ" (2 Corinthians 10:5). Week by week, as they bring their thoughts into obedience to Christ, the women blossom like delicate flowers and the fragrance of their lives reaches out to others (2 Corinthians 2:14-16).

Let's take those ten pieces of ungodly advice and see what God's counsel would be:

1. Do not leave your husband.

God loves your husband and wants him to love Him more than you do. Instead of leaving, ask God what He would have you do to change the situation. This might be as simple as showing affection, fixing his favorite meal, changing the furniture around, getting a new hairdo or losing some weight. Learn how to change some attitudes. Learn how to smile again. Tease, laugh and play. Determine to make love the way he wants to. The knowledge of God's Word will set the wife free to enjoy sex with her husband. Nowhere in His Word are there prohibitions for the ways of married lovemaking (see 1 Corinthians 7:4, Hebrews 13:4, Proverbs 5:18-19). Ask God to give you a giving and forgiving attitude.

Some respond to such advice with the complaint, "Why is it always that the woman has to change?" My answer is this: "You are the one who wants to improve your marriage and it has to start some place. So take the initiative. When you begin to change you will see results in his life, too."

God says in His Word that the believing wife should not leave her husband. 1 Corinthians 7:10 says this explicitly. I tell the women that when God says "no" or "yes" about something in His Word, they shouldn't have to "pray" about what is His will. It's already in black and white. God wants them to stay with their husbands and He will teach the wives something very special through this problem.

2. Don't kick him out of the house.

The house is not "your" house. The wife should not call all the shots. If a husband is doing something the wife disapproves of, she should try to find out why he does what he does. Perhaps he drinks against his wife's wishes. She shouldn't tell him to go elsewhere to drink. Instead, she should love him and build him up. She should strive to improve communication with him. She should encourage him to talk about his feelings, joys and disappointments, then show him through her love and encouragement that she wants to meet his needs. He may continue to drink but God will give grace for every trial (2 Corinthians 12:9). The wife can let God love him through her. 1 Corinthians 13:4-7 (TLB) tells the qualities of that love:

> *Love is very patient and kind, never jealous or envious, never boastful or proud, never haughty or selfish or rude. Love does not demand its own way. It is not irritable or touchy. It does not hold grudges and will hardly even notice when others do it wrong. It is never glad about injustice but rejoices whenever truth wins out. If you love someone you will be loyal to him no matter what the*

cost. You will always believe in him, always expect the best of him, and always stand your ground in defending him.

3. Don't be concerned about who is right, and who is wrong!

Love costs. Sacrifice is painful. Love is not boastful nor does it need to be proven "right." Jesus was "right," but He was willing to leave heaven's glory to take upon Himself our likeness in order to die and rise again to give us life. He could have said, "They got themselves in that mess. Let them wallow in it." Instead:

God, who is rich in mercy, for his great love wherewith he loved us, even when we were dead in sins, hath quickened us together with Christ,(by grace ye are saved). (Ephesians 2:4-5)

Most men say that their wives never admit to being in the wrong. In my opinion, we women do tend to think we are always right. If many men feel this is true (though they very rarely say so to their wives), it would be wise for us to consciously work at changing this weakness.

4. Do not go home to your folks!

The Bible says we are to leave our fathers and mothers and cleave to our mates (Genesis 2:24, Matthew 19:5). Someone has said, "You can never 'go back.' ". I believe this is true. We made a commitment to our husbands in our wedding vows. We are to stay with him and work it out. I am *not* saying that a woman should stay with her husband and be miserable for the rest of her life. I *am* saying that a wife who follows God's plan will have joy and fulfillment she would never know if she were out of God's will.

5. Do not get a job and live as you want.

A homemaker is one of the most important people in the world. If you are a homemaker your responsibilities and challenges are tremendous. The old saying, "The hand that rocks the cradle rules the world," is true. The most enjoyable, satisfying place in the whole world can be your home. You have the privilege of seeing that your family is well-fed, that the house is orderly and as serene as possible. A well-organized homemaker can handle these numerous and varied responsibilities and still have time to be involved in other wholesome or profitable activities outside the home. Bible study provides many creative and fulfilling opportunities to develop further in areas of leadership, organization and administration plus inter-personal relationships. Often husbands are quite pleased with the way a Bible study involvement encourages his wife to mature as a Christian woman.

I thank the Lord that I have had the privilege of being at home when our children came from school and needed someone to tell their troubles to. And I am grateful that my evenings are free from the need to get ready to go to work the next day. That means I can be with my husband or play and share with our children.

You are not "just" a housewife! You can have a fulfilling career as a homemaker, the one who creates the atmosphere of the home. Yes, I know that all mothers cannot be at home. But my heart aches for the people who care more for "things" than for people. The world says you have to work outside of home as a status symbol, or to fulfill your greatest potential, or to keep up with the Joneses. But the women who work for these reasons are many of the ones coming to me with marital problems. If you must work to put food on the table, please do not work a different shift than your husband. Your time together is very important. Many couples pass each other coming and going, and then wonder why one or the other decided to walk out on their marriage.

If, financially, you really do not *have* to work, talk to your husband, telling him you need and want to be at home. Tell him you love your home and want to have more time to be with him and the children. Being a homemaker is as important as any job you could hold. You may have to forego "things," but your rewards in the long run will be far greater. Your time at home will be invested in *people*. Remember that Jesus said, "A man's life consisteth not in the abundance of the things which he possesseth" (Luke 12-15) — but, "By this shall all men know that ye are my disciples, if ye have love one to another" (John 13:35). If you do choose to be a "keeper of the house," be sure to make your time count. Your husband will not like it if you are running around all day or constantly on the telephone.

6. Do not, as the wife, try to be the head of the home.

Ephesians 5:22 is clear on that: "Wives, submit yourselves unto your own husbands, as unto the Lord." Even if you think your husband is incapable of leading, let him do it and allow him the privilege of failing without your saying, "I told you so." Allow him to make decisions. When children ask questions at the dinner table, let him answer. Wait, asking God to help you keep quiet. Practice James 1:19: "be swift to hear, slow to speak, slow to wrath."

The paradox that many women face is that they want their husbands to lead, yet these women do not want to give up their "rights." To become submissive wives, as God would have them to be, they need to ask God to show them where they have wrongfully been leading in the home. Remember that your husband will not want to be the leader in spiritual things if he is not allowed to be the leader in your love relationships, with the children, and in financial and other decisions. Two cannot lead a home any more than two can be President of the United States at once. Two heads in one home make a two-headed monstrosity.

God says in Colossians 3:18, "Wives, submit (adapt) yourselves unto your own husbands, as it is fit in the Lord." 1 Peter 3:1 expands on this: "Likewise, ye wives, be in subjection to your own husbands; that, if any obey not the word, they also may without the word be won by the conversation (behavior) of the wives." These passages do not say that a wife must be a door mat. Instead they teach, as we have observed many times, that the husband will become a loving leader when his wife allows him to be free to make the choice. The phrase, "likewise, ye wives," in 1 Peter 3:1 is the woman's encouragement to be submissive even as all Christians are to be to every human institution (1 Peter 2:13-17), as servants are to be to their masters — both the reasonable and the unreasonable (1 Peter 2:18-20), and as Christ was to the injustices heaped upon Him (1 Peter 2:21-25). Wives must imitate the mind of Christ, accepting suffering and committing their needs to God, the righteous Judge.

As wives we need to be a "help meet for him" (Genesis 2:18). The word "meet" means suitable or fit for him. We are to talk things over with our spouses. We can offer our opinion. But as the president of the family corporation, the husband makes the final decision. We have the honor of serving as vice-president. That unique place, too, is necessary to the family unit.

7. If you get a divorce you will lose far more than you will gain, financially or in any other way.

Many divorcees in our Bible study say that they are sure they would not have been divorced if they had known then what they know now of God's plan for husbands and wives. They are sure their marriage could have been saved. It is true that God permitted divorce in cases of adultery, but this concession was granted because of the "hardness of your hearts" (Matthew 19:8). God wants believing wives to forgive their husbands and try to find out why a divorce was suggested. If there was another woman, the wife should find out why the husband felt he needed her. Did she listen more? Talk less? Admire more? Love better? Proverbs 5:18-19 says a man's own wife should meet those needs:

> *Let thy fountain be blessed: and rejoice with the wife of thy youth. Let her be as the loving hind and pleasant roe; let her breasts satisfy thee at all times; and be thou ravished always with her love.*

Note that both the husband and the wife should "let."

Many women have come to me saying a divorce was imperative

"before he takes everything." But through counseling they learned to trust God rather than act in fear. As the wife began doing what she had neglected to do, God did the rest, working miracles.

8. The children's own daddy is special. God made him special.

Proverbs 17:6 says, "the glory of children (is) their fathers." Encourage the children to love and honor their father. Make his homecoming the most important event in the day. Praise their daddy in his hearing.He will basically become what you tell him he is. Some fathers will seem too lenient, and some too strict. But rather than trying to "alter" the man they wed at the altar, wives and mothers should let him be himself. They need to commit their husband to God, so God can be free to correct him. God will moderate him with experience and freedom to make decisions. Along with this, mothers need to trust God with their children.

9. Don't walk out of the room when you are having a disagreement.

Problems are solved by learning to face them, not by attempting to run out on them. Proverbs gives us some good suggestions on communication:

> *She openeth her mouth with wisdom; and in her tongue is the law of kindness. (Proverbs 31:26)*

> *Only by pride cometh contention: but with the well-advised is wisdom. (13:10)*

> *Pleasant words are as a honeycomb, sweet to the soul, and health to the bones. (16:24)*

> *A soft answer turneth away wrath: but grievous words stir up anger. (15:1)*

> *He that answereth a matter before he heareth, it is folly and shame unto him. (18:13)*

> *It is better to dwell in the wilderness, than with a contentious and an angry woman . . . . Whoso keepeth his mouth and his tongue, keepeth his soul from troubles. (21:19, 23)*

We encourage the women to read good books on communication and to learn how to discuss without anger. We urge them to listen deeply to what he is saying, asking themselves, "Why does my husband feel this way?" It is best to identify the problem and discuss it without bringing in other problem areas. To encourage their husbands to talk, women should clarify the issue by saying, "Did I understand you correctly? I want to know what and how you think. I care about you." A wife should be prepared to do what her husband suggests or she will find that he won't communicate further. Some call it fair fighting. God says, "Speak the truth in love" (Ephesians 4:15).

10. Do not withold your love from him if he has another woman.

The world may say, "Leave him," but I say, "Love him." He turned to the other woman because something was lacking in the relationship with his wife. I am not saying that she is totally at fault, but I am saying she can be a big part of the healing. No husband should "need" to go to another woman for love and admiration. The wife should ask God to give her a forgiving spirit (Ephesians 4:31-32) and fill her with His love for her husband. She should think of five things that she likes about him and begin today to tell him. If she can't think of any, she should ask God to help her see his good points. If the wife doesn't, "she" will. But the other woman has nothing God cannot give the wife, and the wife has the advantage.

Those who still have husbands should ask God to keep their hearts tender to the husband's needs. They should not wait until they have a problem. A book that has been a great help to many is *The Act of Marriage* by Tim and Beverly LaHaye (Zondervan, 1976). Women whose husbands have read it report they are delighted with it, too. Learn together to be lovers. Say to your husband, "Honey, I want to learn to be a good lover. Please teach me, but please be patient with me. I learn slowly." This will encourage him, too.

Most of the women who have come with problems have been reunited with their husbands because they have been obedient to God's Word. Many of the husbands have received Christ. Now together they have the Holy Spirit in control of their lives to help them work out problems which all Christian marriages have.

A well-known family counselor once said that all marriages have basically the same problems. It's just that some couples work them out. How are you responding to your problems? Are you letting God teach you? Are you trusting Him to work out His perfect will in your life? Remember, He uses problems to teach us to rely on Him and trust Him. The better we learn these truths in our own marriages, the better counselors we will be.

PART II — SUGGESTIONS FOR COUNSELING IN A GROUP

As our Bible study began to grow in numbers, I'd often find one to five women waiting for me after the lesson, seeking personal counseling. As I talked with them separately, I found myself turning to many of the same

Scriptures and giving the same basic homework. Rather than trying to find more counselors to reach this increasing number of women, we felt these truths could be shared with more in a group situation. So we started a marriage problems class as a "second hour" group.

The number of women we could help increased as some brought neighbors and relatives experiencing marital problems. Several women received Christ through the class each semester. We especially delight in watching physical changes in the women over the semester. On the first day their walk is usually slow and heavy, their brows furrowed, their faces colorless. They are fearful and timid, sometimes hostile. But as God begins His work in them, they begin to sit taller. Pinks return to their cheeks and their eyes sparkle. They begin to look much lovelier as they allow their lives to be transformed from the inside out. Everyone in the group notices with joy the changes from week to week.

If you decide to begin such a class in your Bible study I have three basic suggestions.

1. *Pray for the right leader.* She should be a maturing Christian who loves people and relates well to them, and enjoys a good relationship with her husband. She must have a growing faith in the Word of God and in His power to change lives. She must believe that with God nothing shall be impossible (Matthew 17:20, 19:26, Mark 10:27 and Luke 1:37), but that without Christ we can do nothing (John 15:5). She should be experienced in counseling on a one-to-one basis. As she considers taking on a class which may grow to 20 or 30, she should recognize that God must do the work: "Not by might, nor by power, but by my Spirit, saith the Lord of hosts" (Zechariah 4:6). His Holy Spirit will do the counseling through His Word.

The counselor must love the sinner, but not her sin. The account of the woman at the well (John 4:6-42) shows that Jesus loved and accepted this woman even though He knew her sin. People need to be prayerfully brought to the place of recognizing their sin and confessing it. If they allow their sin to continue unconfessed, they will remain miserable and waste time and money on counseling. Proverbs 28:13 says, "He that covereth his sins shall not prosper: but whoso confesseth and forsaketh them shall have mercy."

2. *Pray for assistants for the leader.* It is very important to have godly women to help, especially if your group is large. One of the assistants should keep attendance records and the other check the memory verse for the day. It is a blessing to have these women support the leader and the group in prayer and also help in the sharing time. The assistants should be available after the lesson for more counseling. As co-counselors these assis-

tants should be in harmony with the leader's philosophy of counseling. I have had the privilege of having four godly women as assistants in my group. Their help was invaluable. We found it most successful to divide the roll into four groups, with each assistant taking a fourth of the women to pray for and telephone. This takes the extra load off the leader. She still directs the class discussion, however, and handles counseling of extra-troublesome problems.

3. *Have the women write down their problems.* The first day in class we ask each woman to write on a 3x5 card the specific problems she has in her marriage and home. This helps us to know what their problems are and aids us in praying for each woman.

We arrange chairs in a circle to encourage group participation. Each woman wears a name tag with her first name only. From the first day they become concerned for each other. From week to week they rejoice in answers to prayer as different ones share what God is doing in their lives and homes. We also have luncheons including sharing times once a month in the home of one of the women. At the end of the semester, some do not feel ready to leave. They are invited to stay. The rest, hopefully, go on to other interest classes because they feel that God has met their need, and has touched their marriages with His healing power. We encourage women to stay in the group the whole semester even though their marriages are improving.

Probably the slowest, hardest lesson for a woman to learn is that she is a definite part of the problem. Usually on the 3x5 card she will write, "My *husband* is an alcoholic, *he* is too strict, *he* isn't a good lover, *he-he-he.*" It takes a while before she sees herself as God sees her. And that may hurt. But only after God breaks us can He begin to rebuild us, constructing into our lives the "fruit of the spirit" — "love, joy, peace, long-suffering, gentleness, goodness, faith, meekness and temperance" (Galatians 5:22-23). When a husband sees these qualities emerging in his wife's life it won't be long before he will want the same thing.

We encourage women to go home after Bible study and tell their husbands, "Honey, I learned something today. I learned that I have been wrong." And — she is to tell him *how* she has been wrong. Nothing could please a husband more than to know that God is on his side, or that his wife is seeing she is wrong in some areas!

EIGHT BASIC PROBLEM AREAS

I have found marital problems lodge in eight basic areas:
1. *Communication* ("He won't talk to me").

2. *Husband's disinterest in wife, children or home.*

3. *Husband's drinking problem.*

4. *Husband's extramarital affair* ("I can't forgive him, although he wants to come home." Or, "How can I win him back?").

5. *Children* ("His, mine and ours" or, "He is too strict, lenient or unloving").

6. *Sexual incompatibility* (this is the number one complaint of men).

7. *Financial problems.*

8. *Other problems, including in-laws, priorities and organization, and depression.*

Many of these problems overlap. The various categories of solutions to marriage problems cannot always be isolated. For example, when the wife begins to show her husband more interest, love and appreciation, he may in turn respond with a greater interest in her. When she stops nagging about where he goes and with whom, he feels free to stop drinking without feeling that he is complying with his wife's wishes. (*He* wants to make the decision when and if he will stop drinking.) When he is allowed to make more of the decisions he may begin to show more attention to the children. There will be better communication as the atmosphere relaxes and trust grows. The husband and wife will be able to talk over financial problems and will be less likely to act and react in haste or to punish the other. Their love life will begin to deepen and grow as God has planned, and they will begin to find great delight in one another as the wife begins to respond to the husband. In-law resentment will lessen, depression lift, and attitudes about organization and priorities improve, as other areas of conflict are resolved. In fact, a wife will see the husband begin showing an interest in getting to know her God. He may even accept a "date" with her to an evening potluck dinner or a couples' evening Bible study. Best of all, he *will* want to know her God.

"WHAT DID THE LORD DO?"

Each week I open the marriage problems class something like this: "Good morning! How was your week? What did the Lord do in your home? Are things any better? Tell us about it." Sometimes the response is slow, but it comes. Someone might say, "I can't understand it but my husband is being nicer to me."

Another may say, "My husband and I made love this week for the first time in a long time, and I didn't even have to initiate it."

The women spontaneously share in this manner until, inevitably, someone will say, "But that doesn't work with my husband," or, "I just can't understand why my husband does this." I ask questions to draw her out and our discussion topic for the rest of the hour emerges. There is no pre-planned topic. We find that this method is far better than a leader saying, in effect, "Wait. We can't talk about your problem. We must talk instead about what we have planned."

As we all listen to the problem discussed I may say, "What do the rest of you see as a factor contributing to the problem?" I have been amazed and thrilled at the insight many of the women have. It is so special when one will speak up and say, "I can identify with her, because that was my problem. But this is how God worked in my life and how I changed. This is what happened as a result." It is good for all of us to hear how other women have learned to cope with their problems. Although there are times when we disagree, we do not tell the woman sharing that she is wrong. Instead, I may say, "What does someone else see?" *Then* we gently bring the discussion to God's Word. We open it right there, each week, and discuss what God says about this subject. The women underline the verses and/or put a piece of paper in the spot, so they can look it up later. Before long they have the privilege of sharing God's Word with a friend who may be having the same problem that God helped them through.

My assistants have a good sense of timing. At just the right time — led by the Holy Spirit — they share what they have learned, too.

The women grow to love each other as they share their problems and learn to encourage and pray for one another.

As a good suggestion presents itself, we all take that as our assignment for the week. We also take a key verse to memorize. Leaders are not exempt from doing the homework and memory work: we, too, must keep our home lives loving and exciting! The following week we begin our sharing time by telling the results of putting to practice the homework and verse.

Some women may come to our Bible study for years, remarking, "The references to the home are not for me. My marriage is perfect." But we know there is no such thing as a "perfect" marriage and we have sadly watched some of these women suddenly find their marriages in trouble. The cautions we discussed were the areas they allowed to slip. Many times they find out in time. But occasionally, they "see" too late, and their husband has left.

As I mentioned, marital problems lodge in eight basic areas. Briefly I would like to take each problem area and give a typical case, and the homework and Scripture we assigned for each.

1. Communication

One of the women in the class said she and her husband had little, if any, communication. As we discussed this, someone suggested that she get up and fix breakfast for her husband. One of the women shared how this had been her love gift to her husband and she saw the walls of distance begin to melt. "I didn't like to get up early and my husband knew it." she said, "so he told me to stay in bed. He said he didn't like breakfast anyway." One night at a party she overheard him tell someone, "My wife never gets up and fixes my breakfast." Instead of retorting, "Why, you told me you didn't like breakfast and that I should stay in bed because I needed my sleep," she went to work on the assignment. To her surprise, the first morning he thanked her. Even though he had to leave at 5 a.m. for work, she struggled up and eventually found that their time together was a real delight.

From this discussion we took the homework of getting up and fixing our husband's breakfast if we hadn't before, even if it was only juice or coffee. We emphasized that the women should look nice that time of morning, too — getting dressed (or at least getting a new bathrobe if theirs was shabby) and combing their hair. (Many of the women said when they got a new bathrobe their husbands told them how much they hated the old rag they were wearing. Women who can't afford a new bathrobe should be sure the old one is mended and clean.) It is important to your husband how you look when he leaves home for work. How does he last remember you? Remember, there are some very cute gals "out-there" who are not in an old bathrobe.

Each of us is encouraged to be pleasant, smile and talk little for these breakfast times. By "talk little" we do not mean the wife should clam up, but that she should refrain from always having a remark or comeback. The wife should walk her husband to the door, give him a big kiss and tell him she can't wait for him to come home.

We also encourage the women to go for walks or sit out in the yard with their husbands. They should listen, ask some questions, and show an interest in his childhood, boyhood dreams, favorite dog, favorite color and so on. "He is a very special person," we say. "Get to know him."

A good book to read about communication is *Communication: Key to Your Marriage* by H. Norman Wright (no relation to me), published by Gospel Light (1974).

The verse to memorize with this assignment is usually Proverbs 15:13: "A merry heart maketh a cheerful countenance: but by sorrow of the heart the spirit is broken."

Other good verses for this problem are James 1:19; Proverbs 15:1, 15:28, 18:13, 21:9, 19 and 23; and 31:26.

2. Husband's disinterest in wife, children or home

Sometimes this problem becomes apparent as the wife says, "My husband is a Christian but he will not take the spiritual lead or show a real interest in the home."

We discuss why a man might not want to take the lead:

—He may resent the way she "runs" to Bible studies, church or retreats "all the time."

—He might feel he cannot lead as well as his wife. She may even unknowingly put him down in other areas as well as this one.

—She may not be willing to follow his leading. For one to be a leader, he must have a follower. We encourage her not to nag her husband about going to church, having family devotions or spending more time with the children. (My husband Jim says the first time I suggest something is not nagging. Nor is the second, because he may have forgotten. But the third time *is* nagging.)

We often encourage the women to ask the Lord in prayer to show them how they may be leading in the home.

Little things count. Perhaps the wife has been the one at the table to say who will pray. Who is leading? The wife! Instead, she might say, "Honey, who would you like to have lead in prayer?" He may say, "Oh, I don't know. You do it." Then do it, because you will be following your leader. The next night, wait. The husband may say, "Well, aren't you going to pray?" She may answer, "I was waiting for you to say who you wanted to lead in prayer." He may call on you or little Johnnie for the next 20 days. But that's okay. He is leading.

Another place where women usually lead is in decision-making for the children. For example, when a child asks at the dinner table a question like, "May I go to the park tonight?", often the mother answers before the father has a chance. I believe women have a tendency to do this for two reasons:

a. They may not like his usual answer, so they give theirs first.

b. They think he takes too long to answer, or wonder if he is even listening. We suggest that for the coming week (and the rest of our lives) all the wives *wait* for the husband to answer. He *will*, if we don't. Don't ask, "Did you hear the question?" Wait. It's hard, I admit. But wait and let him answer. And stick by what he said. Tell the children, "Dad is the head of our home. What he says, goes." You won't believe the change in your husband. He will begin to take leadership and you will be amazed at his ability.

The homework then becomes two-fold. Wait for him to lead in prayer time, if you are in the habit of choosing who prays. Also, wait to let him answer the children. (This is true even if he is their stepfather.) The children must treat him with respect. If you don't, they won't.

The Scripture memory assignment may be Galatians 6:9, Proverbs 11:22 or Proverbs 31:11-12.

3. Husband's drinking problem

Many times the problems center in the husband's drinking. A wife may complain, "He's gone all the time", or, "He's out late every night."

Our discussion comes around to how we wives must make coming home a thing of joy. Don't interrogate him: he doesn't want a "mother" for a wife. We suggest that the women set a pretty table, including a tablecloth and flowers. They should fix his favorite meals, smile and be pleasant. (Mealtime becomes the focus of attention because resentment has also made the meal an unhappy occasion rather than a time for family togetherness.)

The very next week as we gather to share the results of doing the "assignment," the room bubbles with excitement. When I ask, "How did your husband react when he came home and saw the pretty table and his favorite meals?", I hear comments like this:

"He asked me who was coming to dinner. When I told him no one he said, 'Then why the pretty table?' I answered, 'Just because I love you.' He was so pleased that he came home early the rest of the week, to see if I had changed. Our relationship is so much better."

"My husband didn't stay out all night drinking. I can see that the woman *is* the atmosphere of the home."

Testimonies like these occasionally prompt joyous laughter and the women often clap their hands. When this happens I am reminded of Isaiah 55:12: "For ye shall go out with joy, and be led forth with peace: the mountains and the hills shall break forth before you into singing, and all the trees of the field shall clap their hands. Praise the Lord. He *is* at work.

The main thing that has worked for the women is refraining from asking their husbands how many drinks they had or with whom. It works. But be consistent. Don't just "try it out." Do it as unto the Lord. Many of the men have come to know the Lord because the wife got off the husband's back – and came to his side. Jesus said it's not what goes into the mouth that defiles a man, but that which comes out of the mouth via the heart (Matthew 15:11-20). If what comes out of a wife's mouth is resentment, hate and bitterness, this is as bad or worse than what goes *in* a husband's mouth.

Besides Matthew 15:11, other good verses to memorize are Isaiah 26:3-4, 1 Corinthians 13:4-7 and Philippians 4:6-7.

4. Husband's extramarital affair

Often we hear this sad story: "My husband is unfaithful. He has a girl friend. He says he wants to be free. Should I let him go or try to win him back?"

Before we give an answer or suggestions, we discuss as a group some of the reasons a man would want another woman. The women begin to see that when things are not right at home, Satan can begin to tempt a husband to be unfaithful. We discuss what we can do to make things better at home. First, we need to go to God for strength and His love for our husbands. We need a forgiving spirit (see Ephesians 4:31-32). We need to let him know we love and forgive him and want him to stay. Then, we need to begin to show him that love by actions.

In 1 Corinthians 7:13-16 God tells the believing wife not to leave her husband but to love him and meet his physical needs (1 Corinthians 7:3-5). In doing so, we have found, he will want to stay. He is uniquely set apart because he is married to a Christian. Eventually he will want the Lord.

Many women think that because the Scripture says, "if the unbelieving depart, let him depart," they should let him go without an all-out effort to win him back. But he is your husband, the father of your children. God has said, "For this cause shall a man leave father and mother, and shall cleave to his wife: and they twain shall be one flesh. Wherefore they are no more twain, but one flesh. What therefore God hath joined together, let no man put asunder" (Matthew 19:5-6).

"How can I win him back?" a woman may ask.

Invite him to dinner (if he has left). Set a pretty table. Some have set a pretty "coffee table" and sat on pillows, wearing *his* favorite gown. You may want to send him a pretty card. Don't say too much on it; "I miss you" is enough. Buy a new nightie. He is your husband. Love him as he has been wanting you to. Get away alone. Share with him how God is showing you that you have been wrong. Be specific in telling how you were wrong. Ask his forgiveness.

Verses to memorize: Ephesians 4:31-32, Proverbs 5:18-19 and 31:11-12, 1 Peter 3:4 and 4:8, Hebrews 13:4.

5. Children ("His, mine and ours" or, "He is too strict, lenient or unloving")

One woman shared that her husband remarked recently that she had never really let him have control of their son since an incident 15 years before, when the boy was two years old. "My husband spanked the boy and I got very upset," she recalled. "For some strange reason, it was okay for me to spank him, but not okay for my husband. I guess I thought he spanked too hard." Now they were having trouble with their son. This wife is finally learning, hopefully not too late, to let her husband lead.

Some of the older women shared how they had failed to let their husbands be the "head" of the home in those early years and have since reaped sorrow.

Over all the protests we leaders encourage the women to let their husbands make the decisions, even though they do not agree with them. Yes, we may (we must!) discuss our feelings, but afterwards we must let him make the decision. We must not try to protect the children from their father, or their father from what the children are doing.

Many of the women say, "But you don't know *my* husband." And we say, "But you don't know our God. He can do anything."

For homework, then, the mothers are to tell their spouses, "I've been wrong. I've been calling the shots. I know it's not my place to run things. I also know that God doesn't want me to be a dominating woman. Please forgive me." Then let *him* lead. Pray for God's grace.

Verses to memorize would be Proverbs 25:24, 23:24-26, and 22:15; and Psalms 127:3-5, 128:3.

6. Sexual incompatibility

Someone once defined "incompatible" as "He doesn't make enough income and she isn't very patable." Jokes aside, this is a very serious area and sometimes the problems are so complex a woman needs someone else's objectivity to see the answer.

"My husband asked me to wear a brief halter and short shorts out on the street," a young woman commented. "I know that God wants us to be submissive to our own husbands, but we are Christians and work with the youth of our church. What do I do?"

We could have begun to attack his "unspirituality," deciding the husband should not be leading the youth because he was not walking with the Lord. But I chose to look at the problem another way.

'Why does he want you to wear skimpy clothes out on the streets?" I asked her.

"I don't know," she said.

"How is your love life?" I asked.

Without hesitation she added, "Oh, it isn't too good right now. We are at church almost every night and come home so exhausted we fall right to sleep. When we try in the morning to love, the baby wakes up and so it has to be very hasty."

After the group discussed possible solutions, I asked, "Do you think he might be asking you to dress like that because he is not enjoying this most important relationship, as God would have him? It seems your husband is not getting to enjoy your body at home because you are too busy. Because his desire is for *you* and not someone else, he asks you to dress this way so he can 'look.' "

We encouraged her to carve out some time for just the two of them to really enjoy one another.

With joy and smiles the next week she reported that "things are going much better. I told my husband what we had discussed and he decided we should stay home that evening. We did and had a beautiful time together."

Several months later I asked her if her husband again asked her to wear skimpy clothing on the streets.

With a big smile she said, "No. We're putting our relationship with each other first and we find we are better able to serve the Lord."

Tina was another who had problems in the physical part of her marriage. One night in bed, after the lights were out, she turned to her husband and said, "I have been the one to say *how* we would love, *when* we would love and even *where* we would love. I didn't trust you. I felt you were not as wise as I am about how we should love. But I learned today at Bible study that I have been wrong. God says that 'marriage is honorable in all and the bed undefiled.' God gave sex to Adam and Eve before they sinned and it is beautiful. God also says I am to submit to my own husband. That is why I have been wrong. Will you forgive me?"

They cried together that night as God began to heal this area of their marriage. And later her husband came to know Christ as his Savior.

When sexual incompatibility is our discussion problem, we make our "homework" taking time for loving — giving this most-needed area our priority and sensitivity. Verses to memorize: Hebrews 13:4, Proverbs 5:18-19, 1 Corinthians 7:3-4.

7. Financial problems

Financial problems loom large in the lives of many couples. Although our group varies greatly economically, each of us needs to learn to live within our husband's income if we choose to be "keepers at home." We must learn to cut corners and make do. In our group we discuss budgeting, trimming wants and even living without credit cards. We share ideas and suggestions.

Women often ask, "How can I keep myself from wanting more money and the things it will buy?" As we turn to the Word of God we see that we are to be "content with such things as ye (we) have, for he hath said, I will never leave thee, nor forsake thee" (Hebrews 13:5). 1 Timothy 6:6 says that "godliness with contentment is great gain." Paul said,

> *I have learned, in whatsoever state I am, therewith to be content.*
> *I know both how to be abased, and I know how to abound: every*
> *where and in all things I am instructed to be full and to be*
> *hungry, both to abound and to suffer need. I can do all things*
> *through Christ which strengtheneth me. (Philippians 4:11-13)*

Do not try to solve the problem hastily by going to work. Trust the Lord. He is trying to show you where to trust Him more. We talk about working out a budget and staying with it. We tell the women to encourage their husbands to take over the money — and then let him. (If he spends heavily, a wife should not try to correct him, because then he will only spend more.) We also tell the women to encourage any bill collector to talk with "my husband, for he is the head of our home." Trust God to work it out. Many have! And the results are tremendous.

Someone once said, "You'll find you can live on less when you have more to live for." Another quote worth remembering is, "You make the living, honey, and I'll make the life worth living." This type of cooperation makes sense.

A most important "don't": A woman who has money other than what her husband earns (from her own job, an inheritance or a gift) should *never* say, "This is my money." You married and became one. It's *"our"* money together.

An assignment for financial problems: talk over with your husband where he thinks you could cut down the spending. Then do it. Tell him you appreciate his hard work for the family. Tell him often how much you appreciate him. Be content to live within his income. Verses to memorize: Hebrews 13:5, Matthew 6:19-20 and 33, Colossians 3:2, Philippians 4:19.

8. Other problems

In-laws. We suggest a wife write a thank you note to her mother-in-law, listing some of the good qualities in her son and expressing gratitude for these. Verses: Genesis 2:24 and Matthew 19:5.

Organization and priorities. We recommend that the women make a list of things that need to be done or changed, putting the most important items at the top. This includes things their husbands have been asking them to do for a long time. Then, they're to do those things! This is a fun assignment. The women's comments are priceless! Verses: Matthew 6:33, Philippians 4:13, Colossians 3:17, 23-24.

Depression. In our discussion we often recommend that the women read Tim LaHaye's book, *How to Win Over Depression* (Zondervan, 1974). Suggested memory work: Romans 15:13, Philippians 4:8.

From week to week we see patterns of indifference, disrespect and coldness begin to break down. Testimonies encourage all the women to pray and work harder. Often a husband will say to his wife, "You're sweeter than you used to be." In fact, the husbands insist that their wives keep going to Bible study — a situation that has become a standing joke for us. "My husband looks forward to Thursdays almost more than I do," one woman said. "And — I am so much happier."

Women are truly learning to love the Lord and His Word. They are learning to love their husbands, children, homes, relatives and neighbors. They are becoming tools of God to change the world. God has promised to heal broken hearts and restore the old waste places (Isaiah 58:12). Through our Bible study and marriage problems class we are seeing Him gloriously do this.

I would like to encourage you to have a class similar to ours, to reach your dear women where they are. Your heart will overflow with God's fullness as you witness the transformation of homes and lives.

I like the way instructions for wives are expressed in the Amplified Translation of 1 Peter 3:1-4:

> *In like manner you married women, be submissive to your own husbands — subordinate yourselves as being secondary to and dependent on them, and adapt yourselves to them. So that even if any do not obey the Word [of God] they may be won over not by discussion but by the [godly] lives of their wives.*
>
> *When they observe the pure and modest way in which you conduct yourselves, together with your reverence [for your husband. That is, you are to feel for him all that reverence includes] — to respect, defer to, revere him; [revere means] to honor, esteem (appreciate, prize), and [in the human sense] adore him; [and adore means] to admire, praise, be devoted to, deeply love and enjoy [your husband].*
>
> *Let not yours be the [merely] external adorning with [elaborate]*

interweaving and knotting of the hair, the wearing of jewelry, or changes of clothes;

But let it be the inward adorning and beauty of the hidden person of the heart, with the incorruptible and unfading charm of a gentle and peaceful spirit, which (is not anxious or wrought up, but) is very precious in the sight of God.

WINNING HUSBANDS TO CHRIST

Christian women can have no greater challenge than being God's type of woman to an unsaved husband. As more women came to our Bible study during its early years, our concern grew for these men who did not know Jesus as Savior. And — for the wives who were not enjoying a Christ-centered marriage.

Some of us decided to set aside 10:30 each morning to pray for these men. We agreed, too, to go into our bedrooms at this time and kneel in prayer, if possible.

Ten-thirty became an important event in my home. My little children would come running when I said, "It's prayer time for the men, kids." All of us would rim the bed as even the little ones would pray for these other daddies by name.

The power of prayer! Within three months seven of these men made professions of salvation. Several made their commitment to Christ at a week-long Gospel crusade in our area. My children were excited to see their prayers for these daddies answered. And we women watched with joy as most of these families began attending Bible-teaching churches and some of the men were baptized. For us it was a living demonstration of Acts 16:31: "Believe on the Lord Jesus Christ, and thou shalt be saved, and thy house."

For all of these men, the change in their lives followed directly the changes they saw in their wives who had attended the Bible study. These changes came about because the wives had decided to give the husbands new wives — *themselves.*

Women may come to the Bible study with many complaints about their husbands. But there is one which leads them all: they want their husbands to care more — and show it. This need has been recognized by professionals, too, such as Dr. Karl Menninger, a well-known psychiatrist and author. He observes, "The chief complaint women have against men is not tyranny, infidelity or parsimony, it is passivity. . . . Men, in turn, wish that women would create the emotional climate in the home that makes caring easy and spontaneous."

"TELL ME YOU LOVE ME!"

Many women complain, "I long for my husband to tell me he loves me. I want him to show affection all day, not just when he wants to go to the bedroom. I wish he would do more around the home and care more for the children, loving and disciplining them. Instead he just sits around passively evening after evening."

But how can women change this pattern by providing the right "emotional climate" for him to care?

God has given us the answer. He wants to give women their hearts' desires, to make their homes a thing of beauty, to see their husbands loving and serving Christ.

The critical question is this: are we willing to do what God might ask?

You may be answering, "Yes, I'd do it . . . if I could." What if I told you that God would not only tell you *what* to do but also give you the *means* to do it? Would you still do it?

At this point many women stop and say, "But why do *I* have to be the one to do something?" But that is sidestepping the question. We are talking about winning unsaved husbands to the Lord and seeing husbands become the loving heads of their homes. The implications of such changes are in questions like these:

Do you really want and desire with all your heart that he come to know the Lord?

Do you really want him to love God with all his heart?

Will you support him if God calls him into a special ministry? God may ask both of you (as He did Bill and Harriett of Chris-Town) to become missionaries. He may want your husband to be a Bible teacher or Sunday school teacher. He may call him to preach. He will call for total commitment.

GIVE HIM A NEW WIFE

If you are prepared to support your husband all the way in any commitment God may call him to, then here is God's solution: *give him a new wife*. God has promised results for yielded women:

> *In like manner you married women, be submissive to your own*
> *husbands — subordinate yourselves as being secondary to and*
> *dependent on them, and adapt yourselves to them. So that even if*
> ***any do not obey** the Word [of God], they may be won over not*
> *by discussion but by the [godly] lives of their wives. (1 Peter 3:1,*
> *Amplified, emphasis mine)*

Now, please don't turn away. You may think that submission is too great a price to pay for your husband to become a Christian. But Jesus paid a much greater price for *your* salvation. He gave *His life*. Isn't that what God is asking of us as wives? To give up our lives for our husbands? Paul said that he could wish himself accursed for Israel that they might be saved (Romans 9:3). What love! God often speaks of the Christian being dead with Christ "unto sin" and alive in Christ to walk unto newness of life (Romans 6). Dying "to self"? Paul says in another place:

> *I am crucified with Christ: nevertheless I live; yet not I, but*
> *Christ liveth in me: and the life which I now live in the flesh I*
> *live by the faith of the Son of God, who loved me, and gave him-*
> *self for me. (Galatians 2:20)*

God is not asking anything of us that He was not willing to do Himself. Praise the Lord: He will live His resurrected life in and through us.

In Old Testament times God designated one special group of liberated slaves as "bond servants" (Exodus 21:2-6) and Deuteronomy 15:12-18). They had been released to become free men. Yet they chose, out of love, to continue serving their master.

"That's too great a price, " you may say.

It's not. The rewards far outweigh the cost.

"But I can't submit to my husband," you add. "If I did he would walk all over me. I'd be a doormat."

IT'S NOT DOORMAT THINKING

Submission is not being a doormat. In her book *To Have and to Hold* (Zondervan, 1975), Jill Renich defined submission as the "God-given attitude which helps a woman to find the balance between being a doormat or a domineering shrew." Yes, your husband may tighten things a little too tight when you first begin to let him make the decisions. But remember, he is new at being the leader in your home and he must learn. Talk things over together, then allow him to make decisions. You will be amazed and pleased at how wise he is. When *he* is allowed to lead — and not the wife — he will learn the balance and the *wife* will be the winner.

The good news is that a husband "may be won by the conversation (behavior) of the wife" (1 Peter 3:1). In her excellent book, *Me? Obey Him?* (Sword of the Lord, 1972), Elizabeth Handford says the phrase "may be won" in the Greek is in the simple future indicative sense. More accurately in English, that phrase is "he *will be* saved." This is one of the promises in God's Word we *can* claim. It's not a matter of pleading for a husband's salvation. 2 Peter 3:9 tells us that "God is not willing that any should perish, but that all should come to repentence." It is *God's will* that a husband be saved.

A wife, though, must be sensitive to the purity of her prayer life, and have faith in God's promises:

> *Behold, the Lord's hand is not shortened, that it cannot save; neither his ear heavy, that it cannot hear: But your iniquities have separated between you and your God, and your sins have hid his face from you, that he will not hear. (Isaiah 59:1-2)*

Sin can keep God from hearing your prayers. Thus we need to confess and forsake sin as we claim His promises for our lives (Psalm 66:18).

PRAYING WITH FAITH

God also told us that if we pray "anything according to his will, he heareth us: and if we know that he hears us, whatsoever we ask, we know that we have the petitions that we desired of him" (1 John 5:14-15). It is a matter of thanking God for the answer *before* it comes. That's faith.

Many years ago, a friend and I began to pray for her father's salvation. We were learning a principle new to us: that we should not plead nor beg for his salvation, but, believing God, thank Him already for the man's salvation. Joyfully, we prayed and believed together. Others had also prayed for this man's salvation. A few months after the friend and I began praying, her father — at Easter time — made the resurrected Jesus his Savior and Lord.

My prayer life and teaching on prayer underwent a radical change through this prayer project. I believe now that the secret to answered prayer is this:

1. Be sure it is God's will that you pray about this (1 John 5:14-15). If he has said "no" about a particular matter in the Word, why pray? We need to *obey* the "no."

2. Pray *believing* (Philippians 4:6-7), thanking Him for the answer before you have any evidence that your prayer is being answered.

3. Begin to live in anticipation (Romans 15:13). Faith is catching!

I see these instructions summarized in Philippians 4:6-7, which says we should be anxious "for nothing; but in every thing by prayer and supplication with *thanksgiving* let your requests be made known unto God. And the peace of God, which passeth all understanding, shall keep your hearts and minds through Christ Jesus."

TRUST AND THANK GOD

Back to the original question: to see your husband become a Christian, are you willing to do whatever God might ask? First, will you dare to trust your loving God by lovingly submitting and adapting to the leadership of your husband? Second, will you begin to pray and *thank God* that He will bring your husband to Himself in *His own time?* (Do not put a time limit on God. He is working in many areas of our lives to bring us all into conformity with His will. See Colossians 1:9-14).

Remember that God will not *make* your husband believe in Him, but He will draw him in an unusual way, for you are loving that husband to the feet of Christ. 1 Corinthians 13:4-7 tells some practical ways to show that love. Few can resist love, especially God's love in their mate. Paul recognized this when he wrote the Corinthian believers and addressed wives of unsaved husbands: "For what knowest thou, O wife, whether thou shalt save thy husband?" (1 Corinthians 7:16).

In the same passage Paul encouraged a Christian wife to stay with her unsaved husband, "if he be pleased to dwell with her" (v. 13). This is a key concept, and women whose husbands want to leave home should ask what changes might make him want to stay. Is there love in the home? Does the wife "respect, reverence, notice, regard, honor, prefer, venerate, esteem, defer to, praise, love and admire" the husband (Ephesians 5:33, Amplified)? With God's grace, a woman should try to make her home a little bit of heaven — and give her husband a taste of what heaven is like. She needs to sweep out the bickering, backbiting, hate and bitterness. She needs to make Christianity so appealing that he will want to spend eternity with other Christians.

LOVING IS FORGIVING

We urge wives to truly begin to allow God to love their husbands through them. We encourage them to forgive their husbands of all they have ever done to hurt the wives (Ephesians 4:31-32). When they do this and begin to manifest the "fruit of the spirit" (Galatians 5:22-23) by "chaste behavior" (1 Peter 3:2), we have seen over and over that the husband *will want her God*. He will hunger for God when he has had a taste (Psalm 34:8) of the goodness of God.

Many homes are filled with hatred, hurts and deep wounds. This need not be. What Francis of Assisi prayed long ago is still true:

Where there is hatred, let me sow love;
Where there is injury, pardon;
Where there is doubt, faith;
Where there is despair, hope;
Where there is sadness, joy.

O Divine Master, grant that I may not
So much seek to be consoled as to console;
To be understood as to understand;
To be loved as to love;
For it is in giving that we receive;
It is in pardoning that we are pardoned;
And it is in dying that we are born to eternal life.

Are you willing to "die to self" (Romans 6) that the life of Christ might be manifest in *you?* The joy and reward of having your whole family united in Christ will be yours throughout all eternity. John said, "I have no greater joy than to hear that my children walk in truth" (3 John 4). Are you concerned about your children? Then love their father. God's great purpose is for children to have their own parents. But if you are remarried, then love the one you are remarried to. Children need stable homes.

LOVE A MATTER OF WILL

Genuine love is not just a feeling — it is a commitment, a decision. Love is in the area of the *will.* David often said in the Psalms, "I *will* love the Lord." Many couples say, "I don't love him," or, "I don't love her." But they *can* love the other. It is important to ask the Lord to give you a love for your husband and then set about to put it into practice.

Love must be unconditional, a love with no strings attached. It is not a matter of, "I'll love you if" or "I'll love you because," but rather, "I love you in spite of." It is a matter of the grace of God.

Pray for God's kind of love: unselfish and totally giving. Watch God work a miracle. Begin today to forgive. Touch, smile, flirt, and above all pray. Make your love life something very special (see Proverbs 5:18-19). It is not too late. God heals longtime marriages, too. Give your hurts to God. He says, "Let *all* bitterness . . . be put away" (Ephesians 4:31); "rather let it be healed" (Hebrews 12:13). With God's help you can begin anew, doing things together. Go with your husband. Radiate God's love. Take your husband's arm and be proud of him. He will become what you tell him he is, so tell him he is a wonderful person. Find things to compliment him on. Thank him for all he has done for you and the children. Many men are no more to their homes than a pay check. Ask him to forgive you for your self-righteous attitude. (Don't expect an immediate, positive reaction. He may be too shocked to know how to react!) Do something that he has asked you to do for a long time and you have not done. Go on. It won't hurt. It will heal.

Remember your wedding vows? They probably went something like this:

> I,_____, *take thee,* _____,
> *to be my wedded husband, to have and to hold, from this day forward, for **better** or **worse**, for **richer** for **poorer**, in sickness and in health, to love and to **cherish**, till death do us part, according to God's holy ordinance, and thereto I give thee my troth.*

This chapter may be the first chapter you have read in this book. If so, I am not too surprised, because many women are interested in how to win their unsaved husbands for Christ. But I hope you won't stop here. There is more on this topic throughout this book. Others have written helpful material, too. Go to your Christian book store and find Christian books on marriage and the family. Read all you can. Live all you read by the power of the Holy Spirit. But, be sure to be discerning. If the book does not agree with God's Word, take God's Word over the book.

Throughout much of Scripture, when one member of the family was saved, God brought the rest of the family to salvation. We saw it in Noah (Genesis 6:18), Rahab (Joshua 6:17, 25), Crispus (Acts 18:8), and the Philippian jailer (Acts 16:31). Our prayers will be with you as you pray, love and wait for your whole family to come to know and love the Lord. They will, you know!

"HONEY, MAY I HAVE A DATE WITH YOU?"

The question is simple and loving:
"Honey, may I have a date with you?"

It's the wife's way of inviting her husband to an evening potluck dinner sponsored by the women's Bible study. For some men this may be the first time they have met a number of happy, friendly Christians or heard a layman tell what his life was like before and after he received Christ. It may be the first time they have heard an outstanding Christian musical group.

Non-Christian men are wary of "preaching" meetings. But those who see positive changes in their wives through the women's Bible study will be curious about the people she is studying and sharing with. So, the husband will probably come. But the decision will be his. We encourage the women to love their husbands, not to preach and not to push. If a husband refuses the "date" (which at $1.50 a couple is a bargain!), the wife should respect his choice. Another time he may come.

We have found the evening potlucks are one of the greatest means of sharing God's love with unsaved men. They're not "preaching" meetings, but they are an evangelistic outreach. At a potluck which attracts about 250 people, we may have 15 to 30 indicate they are making a decision for Christ. We try not to come on too strong. Therefore, we do not call in homes afterwards. But during the potluck we emphasize that a new couple's Bible study will begin the next week and they can get in on the "ground floor" of the study. And many choose to do so.

Many men come to the potlucks as cool as the Arctic icecap about God. They've probably decided, "There is no such species as a 'Christian man.' Religion is just for women and children." When they meet and hear men who love the Lord and have a central place for Him in their lives (amazingly, in *and* out of church!) — well, sometimes it melts that icecap in a hurry.

Christians, too, can be encouraged through the potlucks as they hear a positive testimony for Christ — or even give one themselves — and work together to put on an evening that will exalt Jesus Christ.

WHERE TO HAVE THE POTLUCK

The size of your group will largely determine what accommodations you use for a potluck. A fairly small group might choose a home, to permit closer fellowship. We have had three or four Bible study groups meet at a home for a potluck. This helps them see that others are studying the Word of God together. We do not have special music at these small gatherings, although we usually have short testimonies from the group.

Larger potlucks might take place at condominium club houses, community centers, or private or public auditoriums. Here in Phoenix we used the Western Saddle Club a number of times. We also use church fellowship halls and have held a number of potlucks in one which accommodates 250. Several years ago 440 came to a potluck held in a larger church — and another 100 wanted to come but we'd had to cut off ticket sales. We've decided that a group that reaches over 250 is too large for our purposes. Each group, however, must make its own decision.

PLANNING THE POTLUCK

Name a coordinating committee to pray for the potluck, deciding on its purpose – whether to reach the unsaved or to be a fellowship of Christians. As the committee makes plans they should assign people to the various responsibilities, arrange a place to meet, and contact a speaker they feel would best relate to the purpose of the evening. The speaker could well be a man from one of the evening Bible studies who has become a Christian and is growing in his walk with the Lord.

The speaker's testimony should not be too long. In the past we have suggested that a speaker divide his talk in three parts. He should spend one-third of his time talking of his life and home before he came to know Christ as Savior. The second third should tell how he came to know the Lord, spelling out clearly the plan of salvation. The last third of his testimony should relate what God has done in his life and home since he accepted Christ.

The committee should also name a master of ceremonies (preferably a man from one of the Bible studies) and line up appropriate music. Often ensembles from Christian colleges or churches are good possibilities, but be sure they come on a good recommendation, or hear them *first*.

The tickets should be made up several weeks in advance so there will be enough pre-sale time. Try to keep the price low; reduce food costs by having couples bring two medium size food dishes, or one large one. Realize that many will have to pay babysitters at home, too. We charge about $1.50 per couple. This covers cost of coffee, paper plates, rolls, margarine, napkins, room rent and honorariums for the speaker and musicians. On each ticket should be the time, date and place of the potluck and what the couples should bring. You may want to choose a catchy name for the evening.

Plan a few door prizes. These may be for the couple married the longest and the shortest period of time, or for the husband whose wallet contains most of the items read off by the emcee. Or, you may number each name tag and draw numbers for prizes. We often give appropriate Christian books.

One way to organize a moderate-sized potluck is to put three couples in charge of the major planning areas. Helpers would be assigned to each couple, too.

Couple #1 would be in charge of setting up tables (including tablecloths, decorations, paper plates, silverware and napkins). They should place a stack of 3x5 cards or slips of paper at each table. They would also set up a table for name tags (these are important — make sure the names are printed large enough to be read from a distance). All the name tags can be given out at the door at the potluck, or else included with tickets (although the latter procedure results in some being lost). Plan to sell a few extra tickets because four to ten people usually will be unable to come at the last minute. You may want to give a phone number couples could call just before the potluck if they can't make it. Coffee and tea should be made up early to avoid delay.

Couple #2 should be in charge of the food, taking dishes as people come to the door and setting the food on the serving tables. (We hold back a few dishes to be put out for those near the end of the line.) Make sure you have ample serving space so lines move quickly. For our larger potlucks we tried to have four lines. We do not put desserts out until after the program so there will be more time for visiting.

Couple #3 will have charge of cleanup. With their helpers they will wash up any dishes belonging to the facility, such as silverware, pitchers, sugar and creamers and so on. After the guests have left, volunteers should put up tables and chairs and clean the rooms that were used, leaving them as nice, or nicer, than they were found. This, too, is a place where a testimony can be made for Christ.

THE POTLUCK PROGRAM

We use this order for the program:
- Welcome by emcee (Couples arrive about 6:30; we start at 6:45 p.m.)
- Explanation of serving procedure; prayer
- Serving and dinner
- Door prizes
- Music
- Speaker
- Dessert

After the speaker, and before the dessert, the emcee may draw the couples' attention to the 3x5 cards on the table. Ask them to write a note of "thanks" to those who prepared the banquet, the musicians and the speaker. Encourage them too, to put an X on the card if they are making a decision for Christ. Emphasize the Bible study beginning the following week and tell when and where it will meet. Make sure they understand no one will embarrass them, call on them to pray, or ask them to answer any questions at the study.

Often the new Bible study leader will call the ones who put an X on their cards, to remind them of the study. But he must be careful not to push.

RESULTS OF THE POTLUCKS

We try to have several potlucks a year and through them many men have gotten started in couples' Bible studies. The fellowship and study of the Word have brought many men to Christ.

Frank, for example, received Christ while driving home after the second potluck, and then began attending a Bible study. His Jewish wife Jeannette had received Jesus as her Messiah just one year before in our women's Bible study. Now they are united in Christ and active in a good church.

Al came to several potlucks and Bible studies before he put his faith in

Christ. Since then he and his wife Phyllis have become active in a Bible-teaching church.

Ed, a doctor, came reluctantly to a Bible study a few months ago. He told his wife, Joyce, that he'd come once and only once. As he left the study, the leader, Jim, asked if he'd be back.

"Sure," Ed said.

Then his wife added, "But remember we have a music concert next week." (We women too often speak when we shouldn't!)

Ed replied, "We'll see."

They went to the concert the next week but every week following they came to the study. Ed has an insatiable hunger for the Word — as do most of these men when they have tasted and seen "that the Lord is good." (Psalm 34:8). Ed also made the final decision to have his family attend a Bible-believing church.

We always delight in the comments we hear and read on the 3x5 cards after each potluck. Men have said, "When is the next one?" "Why don't you have one each month?" "My wife and I have never enjoyed ourselves more than we did tonight." "Evenings like this give us something special to look forward to because we are not the oddballs at the party." "Program great! Food delicious! Fee reasonable! Speaker and emcee super!" "Thank you for sharing Christ in a real way with us."

COUPLES AROUND
THE WORD

"Why did I say I'd come?" Todd grumbled to himself as he shuffled behind his wife up the walkway to a couples' Bible study. It was Tuesday night, it had been a hard day, and he'd rather be laughing and sipping with his favorite drinking buddy. He'd only had one drink before coming, and that was hardly fortification.

Todd and Eileen had been married nine years and had three children. Their marriage had soured. Todd had turned to drinking and Eileen to nagging. Divorce was a live option. Then, Eileen came to the Chris-Town Bible study with some neighbors. She accepted Christ and the sweet fragrance of her new life turned Todd's head. As Eileen got into a small group on marriage, Todd noticed the nagging and preaching fade from her life. (It was happening for the other women in Eileen's group, too, as they prayed together for their husbands, turning the men over to the Lord and letting Christ love their spouses through them.)

Only two months after Eileen turned Todd completely over to the Lord, a neighbor shared Christ with Todd and the next evening he asked Christ into his life. But for the next six months Todd's spiritual life stayed in neutral gear. He wasn't studying the Bible and neither was he hearing it taught at his church.

A nagging feeling that maybe he *should* get serious about Christianity probably made him say "yes" when Eileen asked, "May I have a 'date' with you for the Tuesday night Bible study?"

Todd was surprised by what he encountered at the Bible study. The couples there were warm and friendly. No one preached at him. Todd relaxed and even shared a few things we had wondered about. The next week he was back, minus the beer. He had done his lesson and even learned the assigned verse of Scripture.

For the next year and a half Bible study had top priority in his schedule. He plunged into his lessons, memorized assigned Scriptures and other verses, too. He so deepened spiritually that after nine months he took over teaching the class he once grumbled about coming to. Todd and Eileen joined a Bible-teaching church and took on a children's Sunday school class. When "Here's Life, America" campaigns were held in Phoenix, Todd became involved and won many to Christ.

Needless to say, Todd and Eileen's marriage has mended. Todd has had no desire for liquor since the third month he attended Bible study. Their lives have become vibrant and fruitful for Christ.

BIBLE STUDIES A BRIDGE

The story of Todd and Eileen is another of hundreds which could be told of how God is using couples' Bible studies. These informal sessions have proven themselves to be an excellent bridge between the unbeliever or new believer, and the local church. Many will come to a home to study the Bible but will not go to church. Or some may have a "church" (though they rarely attend or profit little from its services) and will not visit another. Sometimes those who attend no church complain, "My parents made me go to church all my growing-up years and there's no way I'm going to go now." Frequently the complaint is, "The church has too many 'don't's' — and far too many hypocrites." Or, someone may say, "I don't need church. I just want to find out about God and about God's love."

These people are not ready for a church. They need first to study the Bible in a small informal group situation. As they do and open up the truths of God's Word, the Holy Spirit will nurture their desire to get into a larger fellowship and seek out a church home.

Home Bible studies foster a relaxed atmosphere of learning and sharing that most people enjoy. They can listen to group discussion without feeling pressured to share. They are not called on to pray or answer questions — they volunteer. Some may be studying their Bibles for the first time, or understanding for the first time the Biblical concepts that have drifted past their ears since childhood. Many Christians in couples' studies have remarked, "This is the first place where I've felt I could ask questions and not feel guilty about showing my ignorance." We've also heard, "Although I went to religious schools, this is the first time in my 39 years I've ever opened the Bible."

KEY IS PARTICIPATION

The key to effective evening Bible studies is participation. Discussion of the week's lesson is led by a man (not a woman; since this is a mixed group). The leader refrains from giving "answers" but instead helps the group learn to find these answers in the Word of God. No one is "put down" for a wrong answer. The leader gently guides the group to the Biblical answer or has them look up other Scripture which will lead them to the Bible's answer. Often behind those asking questions which seem to defy answers are the men who later become Bible study leaders or Sunday school teachers.

Home Bible studies help people learn to pray together. They share prayer requests and promise to pray for each other during the week. No one is asked to pray aloud during the group prayer time but within a few weeks usually all will. Soon the leader will no longer need to "lead" the prayer time. Vital to prayer is sharing answers — and discussing why some prayers are answered with "no" or "wait." New dimensions of love blossom out of the prayer and sharing times. Many times people in the prayer circle will realize they are part of the answer to a prayer need. They'll help each other through financial difficulties, share food, move and get jobs.

Through home Bible studies, many families who had no Christian friends before find a whole new circle of friends. They invite each other for dinner, go on picnics, or go camping together. Some are learning that Christians can be found in churches other than their own.

SIZE AND FREQUENCY OF STUDIES

A home tends to properly limit the size of the group. We found it best to keep the group to about 15. (Later in this chapter we'll discuss what to do when your group begins to grow.) The home can be centrally located, although you will find that some couples will drive a great distance to be part of the group. Different couples can bring refreshments each week; this saves the hostess from this extra work. We serve coffee and iced tea, before and after.

We found weekly meetings best. People *will* be there almost every time. Regular meetings will mean regular attendance. And regular attendance will help people shake off the shells which hinder learning, honesty and close friendships, and which could roadblock a growing experience with God. Regularity will also get a person to Bible study the nights he doesn't feel like it.

Meeting once a week will provide enough time between for couples to do their lessons, but be frequent enough for the group to grow steadily in spiritual matters.

We also found it best to meet year-round. At times breaks in the routine may be necessary, although we saw that breaks have a negative impact on the group. When a couple misses for three weeks, it is easy to miss a fourth. Vacations are usually spaced far enough apart to prevent gaping holes in attendance. If a group, however, finds that most families are taking their vacations during a particular month, they may decide to discontinue for that month.

A good time for an evening Bible study is 7:30 to 9:30 p.m. This allows enough time for 1½ hours of discussion, sharing and prayer, and half an hour for fellowship and refreshments after. The evening ends early enough for people to get home for a good night's rest. The hours are also convenient for most family babysitters.

Each group will need to determine the best day of the week to meet. We found Monday or Tuesday best for us but others preferred Thursday or even Friday nights. Most couples like to keep their weekends free for church, sports, camping and family times. Wednesday for many couples means involvement at church — prayer meeting, children's groups, and so on.

CONTENT OF THE BIBLE STUDIES

How you conduct the Bible study is extremely important. Be sure to study your Bible, not a manual nor a booklet of "church doctrines." Ask your people to refrain from talking about churches and you will eliminate many problems.

We have successfully used the beginning study set in Christian living put out by The Navigators (Colorado Springs, CO 80901). (We have used their 10-book set although they now put out a revised 9-book series.) I appreciate, for example, how the first book emphasizes the Person of Christ, the meaning of eternal life and assurance of salvation. You might also want to consider the 10-book set "Ten Basic Steps Toward Christian Maturity," produced by Campus Crusade for Christ (Arrowhead Springs, CA 92404). In either case, a set of about ten books allows a group to progress methodically through the basic tenets of Christianity.

Make Scripture memorization part of your study program. The Navigators, Campus Crusade, and Bible Memory Association (PO Box 12000, St. Louis, MO 63112) have developed helpful systems of Scripture memory. Or, you may choose your own verse from the evening's lesson.

But encourage the couples to memorize one verse a week. And be sure to check the verse the next week. Those who did not wish to memorize will be learning by hearing the verses quoted. Here again, be careful not to embarrass anyone. They might not come back. but as the group builds up a body of memorized Scripture, you will notice strength come into their spiritual lives.

WHO COMES TO THE BIBLE STUDIES

Don't be concerned about numbers. Love and care for the ones who do come. I remember couples' Bible studies that began with six: the host and hostess, the Bible study leader and his wife, and the guest couple. Yet God was there and blessed their study together. If you have only *one* couple, love them to Christ. Do not embarrass them by putting them on the spot. Remember that as they grow in Christ they may be brought to the point where they could start another Bible study.

You will find that couples will invite friends after they feel comfortable in the group and feel they are getting something out of it. You may want to inform people about the Bible study, too, through announcements at the women's Bible studies (put a list on the bulletin board) or through your church bulletin. Of course, studies should also be announced at the couples' evening potlucks (see chapter 9). Ask God to send the right people — those who need and want the Lord. Remember some will be husbands who are curious about the type of people their wives are studying with. Some will want the answer to the baffling but delightful change in their wives. Be gentle with these men. They are very cautious. Love them to Christ.

LEADERS FOR THE BIBLE STUDIES

The man who leads the couples' studies should love the Lord and His Word, and relate well with people. He does not need to know all the answers, but he should know the Lord and how to find answers to questions he doesn't know. Many men are reluctant to lead a group because they feel their knowledge of the Bible is insufficient. But there is no better way to learn Scripture than to lead others in their search for truth in God's Word. And he will find that many theological questions do not demand answers of seminary precision to bring peace to a questioning heart. If he studies the lesson, checks cross-references and does a few word studies each week, he will be able to learn and lead. The leader is not to be a lecturer but one who challenges people to study and through questions motivates them to find answers. He does not tell people what they can find out for themselves. He lets them go away a little hungry to know more. They'll come back.

The leader should also try to sit with the people rather than stand apart. Have the entire group sit around a table, if possible. They will relate better to one another because they are closer to each other. With their books on the table in front of them, they will also be more alert than if they were scattered throughout a living room, sunk into soft sofas or curled up on cushioned chairs — although this arrangement may sometimes be necessary. Never set up chairs in rows with a leader standing in front. Let the leader be one of the group.

THAT FIRST EVENING STUDY

As couples arrive for Bible study together, a host or hostess should offer them a cup of coffee, iced tea or punch. This helps counter awkwardness for any who are new to the group. Each person who comes should also be given a name tag so everyone is not groping for names all evening. Remember, a person's name is very important to him.

Begin the Bible study on time. If you allow for latecomers, they'll come later and later and waste the others' time. Starting on time will mean quitting on time, and this will help young parents who must pay babysitters. Promptness will also draw attention to the purpose of your Bible study — the study of Jesus Christ and our relationship to Him as found in the Bible.

The first few weeks may be awkward for a leader whose group seems to have paralysis of the vocal cords. This will dissipate, however, as the couples learn they can trust each other and that no one will be put down for "wrong" answers. A leader must be patient and loving, but soon he will watch them unfold and become active in the discussion.

During the first week the leader should take the group through the lesson, question by question, showing them how to study. He should not move too slowly, nor too quickly, but be alert that his group understands what is being said. He should watch that no one dominates the evening, or that conversation strays off the subject. (See chapter 6 on small groups for practical suggestions on leading discussions.)

The women should guard their mouths at the Bible study, waiting for the men to speak first. We found that husbands will share if the wife doesn't talk to much. We encouraged a woman not to act shocked at anything her husband might say. My heart sank every time a woman turned to her husband and gasped, "I didn't know you believed that." Instead, a wife should make every effort to avoid embarrassing her husband in his first attempt at sharing in a Bible study. If she wants him to learn to be a spiritual leader, this is one place where he can learn to assume that role.

Ease the couples into a group prayer time. Have the leader pray the first few weeks. He may, as time goes on, ask someone he knows will not be embarrassed to pray. Keep the prayer time short. At first some of our couples arrived 30 minutes late to *miss* prayer, probably out of fear they might be asked to pray. Fifteen minutes is probably a good length of time to pray after the couples begin to pray as a group. Encourage them to pray for one another during the week, and they will be eager to know how God has answered prayer.

As they get into the Bible study and ask questions, suggest that all look up questions the leader or no one else seems to know the answer to. This might be the time to show them how to use a concordance. Point out the one in the back of their Bible or introduce them to a large concordance (such as *Strong's Exhaustive Concordance* or *Young's Analytical Concordance*) to acquaint them with some of the better resource materials available.

TRAINING NEW STUDY LEADERS

Constantly work at cultivating group discussion leaders. Ask God for an assistant. Then watch for the man who studies more than you assign, who is full of questions and whose life shows a marked growth. Ask him to be your assistant. Discuss with him the purpose of the Bible study. Get feedback from him about the group's response. When you can't be there, allow the assistant to lead. When my husband Jim did this, he found the study group liked his assistant. So Jim suggested that many in the group take turns leading. These men found out they could lead – and they enjoyed doing it. That's great, because that's spiritual multiplication by training!

A group may nurture a second leader within six months to a year. At that time the original leader may want to leave to start another Bible study.

During the past 10 years that he has led this particular type of couples' study, my husband Jim has patterned his leadership on these principles of spiritual multiplication. From the beginning he led with two main purposes:

1. That men and women would come to know Jesus as Savior and begin to grow in their knowledge of Him.

2. That as they learned, they would be introduced to a method of having Bible studies which they could reproduce in groups they might be called on to lead.

Our first group of couples was small enough to meet on our patio. That first summer, radio announcer Larry Wright (see chapter 2) accepted the Lord. Phoenix police sergeant Dick Murphey came, he admitted, "because there was swimming before the study," but soon became gripped by study of the Word. The other men also grew tremendously.

When the women's Bible studies resumed in the fall we announced the couples' evening study. We were thrilled as more couples came — including husbands for whom we had prayed. But we faced a dilemma. If they became a part of the group started at the beginning of the summer they would be three months' study behind. And we felt they needed the practical instruction from three months in "Book 1" of the Navigator series we were using.

Our solution was to divide the group — the concept we had adapted for second-hour groups in the daytime women's study. My husband took the newcomers into the family room and let the original group continue in the living room under Larry, who had matured so quickly spiritually that he was ready to be a Bible study assistant. As more people came, we had to start even another group. Finally, we had four different couples' studies meeting in our house and another home in the neighborhood, each led by a man from the original group.

All the leaders met at 7 p.m. to talk over leadership and doctrinal questions. At 7:45 p.m. we welcomed the couples and had coffee or tea with them. A song and prayer time followed at 8 p.m. Then we broke into groups, coming back after the studies for refreshments.

Eventually, though, we had even too many people for this arrangement and had to divide, dispersing similar smaller couples' studies into other homes. But couples' studies continued to mushroom, and we couldn't train leaders fast enough to keep up with the new groups emerging. We asked Ted, one of our men, to teach a leadership training program. He had good materials but we found that those who could train as leaders were already busy in their own churches and could not take on more. Several responded but did not follow through. We found our best "leadership training," however, took place *in* each group rather than "outside." The men who thought they'd never be leaders could be comfortably eased into leadership as they helped in their own groups. They would make better leaders because they would be less likely to "lecture" (as an "outsider" might) and because they had learned the heart-needs of small couples' groups.

Bill, one of the men in our first couples' study, is typical of men who — probably to their own amazement — became excellent leaders. The night my husband suggested to the group of men that they become leaders,

Bill turned his chair sideways and declared, "Not me." He said he was sure he would never make a leader. We didn't push him — just prayed a lot — and later this opportunity came for him to take a new group into the dining room for a study. I am certain he must have been nervous, but he didn't show it. That group stayed together for more than a year. When some felt that Bill should assume leadership of another group, this former non-leader said, "No, you can't take *my* group from *me!*" And his group concurred. In fact, each of the men in our original couples' study became a leader in his own right. Larry, as I said earlier, became an assistant when only a few months old in the Lord. Later he led a couples' study on his own and in the years since has led many Bible study groups, taught a large adult Sunday school class, and become a sought-after speaker for Christian gatherings. Dick, now a lieutenant with a city police academy, founded CLUE (Christian Lawmen United Eternally), a Christian law enforcement group which was featured in the November 1975 issue of *Decision Magazine*. All of the men from that first group continue to be active in their churches, too.

Bob, who had begun coming to Bible study with the second group of couples, was another who typically responded "not me" when the appeal went out for leaders. Then one Sunday his pastor preached on the need for "availability" rather than "ability" before God. The next Tuesday he and his wife Wilma offered their home for a Bible study and he led a group for more than a year before he and Wilma went at retirement into mission work.

The evening couples' studies born out of the Chris-Town women's study have grown in number throughout the Phoenix area. Many churches have adapted the concept to begin new outreach churches. The concept has also been proven successful in Portland, Oregon, where Pastor Albert Wollen of Cedar Mill Bible Church found studies an excellent way to win many in that community to Christ. In a format similar to our evening Bible study method of reproducing new groups, and adapting it to his situation, Pastor Wollen watched more than 100 Bible studies spring up in West Portland. He has also written two very helpful books on home Bible studies: *How to Conduct Home Bible Classes* (Victor Books, 1969) and *Miracles Happen in Group Bible Study* (Regal, 1976)

Other materials helpful to those involved in group leadership include *A Guide for Leadership Training and Bible Discussion Groups* (Billy Graham Association) and *Lead Out* (Navigators, 1971).

We are convinced of the value of couples' home Bible studies. And in saying this we are echoing the comments of men who came, who shared and studied about the living Lord, and who are glad they did. They say things like this:

"I enjoy interacting with people from various jobs and professions as we learn how to apply Biblical truths to our lives. Hearing how others have applied these truths gives the rest of us ideas and encourages each of us in our own daily walk with the Lord."

"Bible study gives me the tools to be a worker for God in my daily life."

"Evening Bible study has been a tremendous help to me as a baby Christian. I'm not only learning a lot, but I am motivated to study and pray daily."

"The home Bible studies give me a way to casually expose friends I am concerned about to the claims of Christ. The groups also help me study Scripture systematically."

"I appreciate fellowship with other Christian men."

MULTIPLYING BY SUBTRACTION

There's a line in Shakespeare's *Romeo and Juliet* which goes, "Parting is such sweet sorrow." Nothing could be truer for our women's study for the times we've had to say goodbye to key women through moving or dividing. Each time we felt as though the Lord had taken a special part of us and we felt the loss deeply.

But the years have taught us to trust Him — and praise him — for the "adding" and "subtracting" that comes to any group, as well as for the "division" that eventually had to result from our membership multiplication.

ADDING AND SUBRACTING

No one likes to say goodbye. Some people even stay home from the airport to reduce the hurt of saying goodbye to loved ones. Farewells come hard at the Bible study, too, especially when the women are sisters in Christ and in some cases have become closer than our own flesh and blood. They are woven into the very fabric of the group, and losing them is like tearing a thread out of the center of the weaving.

It was especially hard to lose leaders. I'll admit that during the first few years of the Bible study I wondered if God had forgotten us or made a mistake when our leaders moved away. But each time He graciously showed us the change was for their best interest, and also for ours. And He always filled the gaps they left. In fact, God started preparing replacements long before we could even have imagined they'd be needed.

The story of Reathal and Pat is an example of that. Reathal had replaced our first coordinator, Jackie. But the story of Pat, who was to replace Reathal, begins several spiritual generations back. For more than a year one of our older women had been asking prayer that her daughter Bonnie would come to know the Lord. One spring morning of the Bible study, to our delight, Bonnie walked in the door. Everything seemed right for this visit. The room was pretty, the table beautifully arranged, and every woman friendly. Surely she would enjoy Bible study!

As I taught the lesson that day during the first hour I watched Bonnie, sitting in the back row. Her brow was furrowed. I sensed she was angry with me and my message, and I wasn't surprised when her mother later whispered to me, "I think we lost Bonnie."

Silently I prayed, "Dear Lord, please bring Bonnie to yourself. Don't let her turn away."

Later I learned that Bonnie met two friends at the bottom of the stairwell on her way out of the auditorium. "You must come to Bible study with me next week," she told them. "I heard the most exciting things – things I have never heard before." One of those friends was Pat. They did come back. Soon after, both women accepted Christ as their Savior when another friend took them to hear an evangelist at her church.

Pat's behind-the-scenes involvement in our Bible study broadened as she helped in just about every area — kitchen, guest table, nursery. When Reathal's husband was transferred out-of-town, Pat seemed to be God's choice for Reathal's replacement. When we asked her to become coordinator, we found out she'd already discussed the possibility with her husband. And she had his approval to take on the responsibility. This thrilled us since we feel it is important for husbands to approve of any extra work or role their wives take on.

Harriett was another example of how God added a leader when He subtracted one. I'll never forget the day she first came to Bible study. She had just moved from California and while all her furniture had come to Phoenix, her heart was back home with parents and friends. She complained about "this desert land" and her pouting finally reached the point where her husband said, "Either you straighten up by January or I've had it. You can go back to California without me."

Then her cousin Frieda here in Phoenix invited her to the Bible study. She came, more out of needing something to do than of interest in God. Harriett did, however, consider herself a "religious" person. She had joined many church groups and even held offices in them. The message she heard that day at Bible study, though, jarred her.

"Did someone tell you that I was going to be here?" she asked me afterwards. "You talked about my exact problem. You were talking about marriage problems and how many of them stem from bitterness which reached back to the honeymoon. That is exactly when our problems began. And that was 17 years ago.''

That day for the first time, too, Harriett realized that God loved her and wanted her to be His child through faith in Jesus Christ. She saw that through Him and through His love she could forgive her husband and love him. That week she went home and, on her own, prayed to receive Christ.

The Word of God took hold in her newly-stirred heart and she began to grow rapidly. About two years later Harriett became our coordinator. About this time her husband Bill began coming to the couples' evening Bible study and attending a Bible-teaching church. He listened in the studies, faithfully did his homework and memory work, assuming these were evidence that he was a Christian. Several months later as he read Tim LaHaye's *Spirit-Controlled Temperament,* Bill realized he had never personally accepted Jesus as his Savior. That day he did.

The change in his life came slow. Too slow, for Harriett, and she became impatient. She had hoped his Christian growth would be as electrifying as that of some other husbands in the study group. Slowly she learned that God was not going to make her husband a carbon copy of someone else. God wanted a man fully yielded to Himself, growing, and learning to trust and love Him. And that is what Bill was doing, in his own way. Harriett finally let go — and let God have His perfect way in Bill. The long, difficult valleys they were going through would be preparation for something special.

Bill began to lead a home Bible study. Then God began to speak to him about serving with Wycliffe Bible Translators as an accountant. Was Harriett willing to let God lead the family through Bill? Yes. She had learned the hard lesson. They went through Wycliffe's preliminary training, including several months of "jungle camp" in Mexico. Before they could go on to their assignment there was a long, hard period of waiting until their home was sold and their support built up. But finally Bill, Harriett and their teenage daughter Jana were able to go to Brazil to serve the Lord.

When Bill shared his testimony at Bible study a few years ago, he said that Harriett made him feel 10 feet tall by allowing him to be head of their home and by loving him through God. But, he added, "in my eyes Harriett is *nine* feet tall!''

Harriett's successor was to be another woman who found Christ through Bible study — Phyllis. A foot operation kept Phyllis from going to work, so she visited the Bible study with her friend Louise, one of the leaders of our small groups. Phyllis remarked later how strange she felt as she walked in on this group of Christian women.

"I can't remember anything that was said that day," Phyllis recalls, "but I do remember the love everyone had for each other and for me, a total stranger. I came just two weeks when one night at midnight God spoke to my heart and impressed on me that I was a sinner and needed a Savior. I knelt right then by my bed and asked Christ into my life and thanked Him for dying for my sins. It was as though a huge weight fell off my back as I was filled with a new love for God and for people."

Phyllis' husband was saved through one of the couples' evening potlucks and attended regularly an evening Bible study. They are both serving in a good church. Two of their married daughters and their husbands also know Christ.

Meanwhile, Phyllis had been watching Harriett as she busily carried out her responsibilities as coordinator. One day she said, "Harriett, the Lord laid it on my heart to offer to help you." When Harriett and her husband left for their training with Wycliffe, it was obvious that God had been grooming Phyllis to be coordinator. Besides working with Harriett, Phyllis had training as a secretary.

Recently four of us drove to another town in Arizona to help some women there begin another Bible study. As each woman shared a little about herself during a get-acquainted time, Phyllis spoke up from her seat on a kitchen stool by the counter. "I used to spend my time on the neighborhood cocktail bar stool," she admitted. "If anyone had suggested several years ago that I'd some day sit on a kitchen bar stool in Humboldt, Arizona, helping some women start a neighborhood Bible study, I would have thought they were ridiculous."

As she spoke I could only praise God for the saving and transforming power of the new birth in Christ.

MULTIPLYING

Many of our "subtractions" have resulted in multiplication. Women (and their husbands) who found Christ or were Christians needing fellowship – and came and served at Chris-Town — continued to serve the Lord as He moved them elsewhere.

Starlyn, our song leader for several years, moved to California where she and her husband settled in an apartment. Anxious to have a Bible study there, Starlyn went door-to-door in the building, inviting women to come. Six came the first day. That group grew together and many came to know the Lord. Starlyn's husband later felt led to serve full-time in that community as a church's minister of evangelism.

I've watched former Chris-Town women start their own Bible studies all over the United Sates, from Texas and South Carolina, to Hawaii and Wisconsin. Many times they found their communities or neighborhoods ripened by God for a Bible study. When Pat, who'd been our coordinator for 3½ years, moved to Houston, within a month she, four new friends and their pastor were planning a women's Bible study as an outreach to the community. The church had begun several women's Bible studies before, but they were not always successful. But the pastor and Pat's new friends were excited about the Chris-Town plan. Four months later in September they began a full-scale Bible study with second-hour small groups. During the first year, the pastor taught during the lecture hour. Since then, several women have taken the first-hour responsibility. Pat has led the guest group where many women came to know the Lord.

It is hard for us to see the women move away and leave the Chris-Town study because we have shared so much in our lives and homes. But when we see the Lord lead them to start a Bible study in their new area, we are reminded that they are acting out the Great Commission, ''Go ye into all the world and preach (teach) the gospel to every creature'' (Mark 16:15).

While we watch excitedly to see God plant seed groups in other communities, we stand amazed at the growth He allows our Phoenix group. I have worked with study groups of many sizes and find that larger studies have many advantages over smaller ones. God can bless the smallest Bible study possible — two people: one nurturing another to the point where that person can help a third come to know the Lord and grow in Him. It's the principle of 2 Timothy 2:1-2:

> *Thou therefore, my son, be strong in the grace that is in Christ Jesus. And the things that thou hast heard of me among many witnesses, the same commit thou to faithful men, who shall be able to teach others also.*

But God can also use numbers to work out His purpose. These are some of the advantages of a large Bible study:

1. The women feel free to bring all their friends and relatives without worrying whether there would be room for them to sit, or a place in the nursery for their children.

2. Pettiness is minimized.

3. The various group tasks (guest table hostess, book sales, leading small groups, etc.; see chapter 5) enable various women to serve according to their spriritual gift.

4. It is encouraging to be among hundreds of other women who love the Lord, and to find friends your age and interest.

5. The studies through second-hour groups can be more closely tailored to a woman's need.

6. The time and place of the meeting are consistent. There is no need to change because a leader's child is sick (or she is sick). This eliminates panic phoning and planning.

DIVIDING

But growth cannot continue forever. Your nursery may have room for no more children. Parking problems may reach serious proportions. You may run out of chairs. This happended to us at Chris-Town and women began to sit on the floors or tables. Some kept their babies with them, because the nursery was already bulging.

Our study had grown to 650 women in attendance (800 on the roll) when these problems became critical. We wondered whether God was now telling us to multiply by dividing. The prospect was painful, though. We didn't want to part with each other. We had ambivalent feelings, as when a son or daughter marries and moves away. Yet God was showing us that it was time for some to depart — and that we needed to send them on with our blessings.

Division can take place several ways, but it must always be bathed in prayer. As we prayed about it, we noted that a large number of the women were driving into central Phoenix for the study from their homes in the northwest part of the city. Perhaps this was where God wanted another study started.

Second, we prayed about a suggested boundary line. One proposed would take in 150 women. As we went through their names in our files, we discovered that the number included 14 group leaders. This was good but — ouch! — that meant one half of our group leaders would be leaving. In addition, many of these women had been in the Chris-Town group for about 10 years.

But from this group God raised up a teacher and two to be coordinators — one for the functional details and another for the small groups.

We decided to divide the group in January when the new semester started. That gave us three months to train the new coordinators and do other planning. Most of the group leaders decided to continue teaching the same topics they had a Chris-Town. So when the new semester began a few years ago, the new "Valley West Bible Study" started in full force with 150 women, a lecture hour and good variety of second-hour classes.

(Some groups which divide may not be able to have second-hour classes right away. A lecture may be fine for a while, but they should try to include second-hour classes as soon as possible.)

I remember our concern over finding the right person to be the teacher for the new Bible study. But God had been preparing her for years. If you are faced with choosing a teacher, relax. Trust the Lord. You will know her, for God will make it very evident to all of you who she should be. She will have the gift of teaching, although she will feel she is unworthy of teaching. She will have the desire to teach, although she will probably respond, "I'd be scared to death to do anything like that."

For us there was no doubt that Sue Wright was God's choice for teacher. (She is no relation to me, except in the Lord; the way God worked in her life and her husband Larry is told in Chapter 2.) Many came to me as we considered teachers and commented, "Do you know who would make a great teacher? Sue! No other person was suggested although several others could have been possibilities. The women saw in her a definite love for God and for other women in the group. She was experienced. For six and a half of the nine years she had been attending Chris-Town she had led one of the small groups. She spoke often to the large group. She would begin by giving her testimony and then share many truths for daily living from the Word.

God gave further evidence that Sue would be the new teacher even the summer before we began praying about dividing Chris-Town. I was to speak at one of the monthly teaching luncheons we have in the summer instead of the weekly extensive studies. I woke up that morning with a severe back pain and knew I couldn't make the luncheon. I phoned Sue. Could she substitute? Apprehensively, she agreed, and in those few short hours God gave Sue a special message that spoke to every heart there.

Later, too, she apprehensively agreed to become the new study's Bible teacher. But in the months that have followed God has continued to affirm that He indeed chose her. Evaluation sheets from the women have been positive. Husbands, too, have expressed gratefulness for what God is teaching the women through Sue's godly life.

The women continue to root their studies in the Bible. The second year, for example, the lesson series was on the women of the Bible. God used Sue to breathe life into the biographies of these ancient women, making them real and the lessons of their lives contemporary. Sue added insights from Gien Karssen's book *Her Name Is Woman* (Navigators, 1975) but her main text was the Bible.

That the new study continues to reach into women's hearts is confirmed by these evaluations from the women who sat both in Sue's lecture and in the small group studies:

"God has taught me to be submissive to Him, to my husband and to those in authority. Through many trials I have learned to have more patience and to trust Jesus more as my total source of supply"

"I feel the Lord has worked through this Bible study to save my marriage and bring my family closer together. What I've learned here has led me to teach others about the Lord and how good He is to us."

"I think the constant reminders of how important it is to work on our marriages and homes is extremely valuable."

"Since coming here I have become aware of my faults and I try harder each day to be the wife and mother I should. Also, I now feel that being at home can be rewarding. I actually enjoy my home and family now. I find that I no longer need to work outside the home to be important."

"I have really learned that God forgives me and answers prayer. He has made me to be a follower of my husband and not a leader. God made me see that He has made me a woman with a purpose in mind. The Scripture has helped me find the answers to my problems."

Sue admits it was difficult to leave Chris-Town and assume teaching responsibilities for the new group.

"My biggest struggles have been with myself," she says. "The Lord has taught me so much and I still am learning! We now have about 170 to 200 women coming, and there are many needs.

"It was very difficult to leave Chris-Town because we loved the women there so very much, and, of course, Naomi is special. But we are thrilled to see God reach out and bring women to Himself and give them a burden for others. Women are crying out for love, and it is our privilege to tell how much God loves them and then let His love flow through us to them."

One of the most amazing aspects of dividing Chris-Town was realizing God has also prepared the place for this new Bible study to meet. A pastor in northwest Phoenix — right where we wanted to locate — had been praying that a women's Bible study be held in his church! The Lord again showed us that He would never ask us to do anything without providing the means to do it. I was reminded of 2 Corinthians 4:7:

But we have this treasure in earthen vessels, that the excellency of the power may be of God, and not of us.

AN EVER-WIDENING CIRCLE

One summer evening several years ago my husband Jim and I sat in church watching the closing program of the daily vacation Bible school. The fifteen women on the platform had dedicated two busy weeks to these particular children, who now shared their verses and songs.

Jim leaned over to me and whispered, "Honey, how many of those women are coming to your Bible study?

I started counting. One, two, three . . . thirteen were! And, most of them were also leaders in our Bible study. More than that, several had received Christ through the study.

This incident happened when the women's Bible study was only a few years old and some had questioned its worth. But as I watched the program and this living demonstration of spiritual multiplication, I could hardly sit still. Truly God was confirming His blessing on the Christ-Town study. One at a time the women had come to the Chris-Town study, hungered for the Word, and made Christ a real part of their lives. Families were claimed for Christ and spiritually revived. And now these women were ministering to other women and to little children, reaching their corner of the world for the Lord.

Later, several women in the study would move away from Phoenix. But as they trusted God to open up opportunities to start another Bible study, He did.

Sometimes women from out-of-town or state would visit the Chris-Town study and tell me, "I wish we had a Bible study like this back home."

"You should pray about starting one, then," I'd say.

"But how do we go about it?"

More and more women started asking me — and writing me — for the "how." Because I knew I could never answer each personally with all the details they'd need, this book was born.

Perhaps this book has stirred in you a desire to be part of God's plan in reaching others for Christ through Bible studies. Maybe you're already thinking of someone who might be interested in helping you with a Bible study. If so, don't run to the phone. Run first to the *Throne*. Pray. Seek God's will in this most important matter. Lay your burden at His feet. Tell Him your feelings of ambivalence, how you want to share Christ and yet feel inadequate. Then open His Word. He offers promises for the task:

> *I can do all things through Christ which strengtheneth me. (Philippians 4:13)*

> *Now therefore go, and I will be with thy mouth, and teach thee what thou shalt say. (Exodus 4:12)*

> *Be strong and of good courage, fear not, nor be afraid of them: for the Lord thy God, he it is that doth go with thee; he will not fail thee, nor forsake thee. (Deuteronomy 31:6)*

Deciding on a place to meet or choosing lesson material are important to starting a Bible study. But more important is the preparation of your heart. Ask yourself, "Why would I want to have a Bible study?" Then read carefully Isaiah 58. The chapter deals with the true abundant life Jesus spoke about (John 10:10). It speaks also of the "fasting" which honors God — not necessarily a ceremonial abstinence from eating but a continuing quality of life:

> *Is not this the fast that I have chosen? to loose the bands of wickedness, to undo the heavy burdens, and to let the oppressed go free, and that ye break every yoke? (Isaiah 58:6)*

How will you do this? God tells the way: "Not by might, nor by power, but by my Spirit, saith the Lord of hosts" (Zechariah 4:6) The Spirit of God uses the Word of God through the man (or woman) of God to loose the bands of wickedness, undo burdens and let the oppressed go free.

The Isaiah passage, too, tells God's promise to those who spend their time helping others to find Christ and be set free:

> *If you do these things, God will shed his own glorious light upon you. He will heal you; your godliness will lead you forward, and goodness will be a shield before you, and the glory of the Lord will protect you from behind.*

> *Then when you call, the Lord will answer. "Yes, I am here," he*

will quickly reply. All you need to do is to stop oppressing the weak, and to stop making false accusations and spreading vicious rumors!

Feed the hungry! Help those in trouble! Then your light will shine out from the darkness, and the darkness around you shall be as bright as day.

And the Lord will guide you continually, and satisfy you with all good things, and keep you healthy too; and you will be like a well-watered garden, like an ever-flowing spring. (Isaiah 58:8-11, TLB)

We must be ready for this assignment. We must expect that God will do what He has promised. He asks not great ability, but availability. He asks faithfulness (1 Corinthians 4:2). He says He will live through us (Galatians 2:20).

You drop a pebble in the middle of a placid, mirroring lake. The mound where it pierced the water becomes a circle which rolls outward, ever expanding its circumference until that circle is thousands of times larger than the stone which caused it. In the same way, God's Word as it pierces the human heart can launch out in ever-widening circles until it touches every individual within reach with the life-giving message transported by the Spirit of God.

Perhaps you already are part of this great, expanding circle. If so, we thank God for you and your ministry. But if you are not, and have longed and prayed for a minstry with other women, we invite you to be a part of our ever-widening circle.

Someone once said, "The world has yet to see what God will do through a person who is wholly yielded to Him." God says, "Therefore, my beloved brethren, be ye steadfast, unmovable, always abounding in the work of the Lord" (1 Corinthians 15:58).

Christ in us is the hope of glory. The Lord has called on us to "proclaim Him, admonishing every man and teaching every man with all wisdom, that we may present every man complete in Christ. And for this purpose also I labor, striving according to His power, which mightily works within me" (Colossians 1:28-29, NASB).

It's His power — His work. And as we allow Him to accomplish His purpose in our lives the effect can be mighty.

APPENDIX

EXAMPLE DOCTRINAL QUESTIONNAIRE

The following is a four-page questionnaire we ask potential assistant leaders to fill out. It touches the basic doctrinal areas which are also given in our statement of faith, found at the end of this appendix.

We do not ask women to pledge to maintain, or to agree, to a certain statement of faith. But we do evaluate their beliefs through the questionnaire. During our group leadership meetings we discuss problem areas.

NAME _____   DATE _____

ADDRESS _____   PHONE_____

PLEASE GIVE SCRIPTURE REFERENCES WITH YOUR ANSWERS.

I CONCERNING THE WORD OF GOD:

   1. Is the Bible inspired? _____

                    (At least 2 verses please)

   2. Has God given us any other sacred writings? _____

   3. Do you feel that this book, written so many years ago can still be taken as authority in matters of life and conduct? _____

   4. Why can't some people understand the Word of God? _____
       _____

   5. How can we judge all religious teachings, as to whether they are correct or not? _____

   6. What is the gospel that Paul preached? _____
       _____

II CONCERNING THE GODHEAD:

1. Do you believe in the Trinity? _____ Why? _____
   _____

2. Do you believe that the Father, Son and Holy Spirit are distinct persons, each with His own office and yet co-equal? _____
   _____

III CONCERNING THE FATHER:

1. Is God the father of everyone? _____
2. Does the Bible teach that God had a beginning? _____
3. Does the Bible teach that God the Father has a body? _____
   _____
4. Is God limited to one place? _____
5. Give a word definition for these words:
   a. Omnipotent _____
   b. Omniscience _____
   c. Omnipresent _____
6. Does God have some or all of the same emotions that we experience? _____ Does God —
   a. love? _____
   b. grieve? _____
   c. rejoice? _____
   d. sorrow? _____
   e. fear? _____
   f. faint? _____
   g. sleep? _____
   h. hate? _____
   i. feel jealousy? _____
   j. feel bitterness? _____
7. Tell 5 things you know about God's love.
   (1) _____
   (2) _____
   (3) _____
   (4) _____
   (5) _____

IV CONCERNING JESUS CHRIST:

1. Did Jesus have any part in the creation of the heavens and the earth?
   _____

2. Did He have a beginning? _____

3. Was He the Son of God with no earthly father? _____

4. Did He live a sinless life? _____

5. The Bible says He arose again the third day. Was it a bodily resurrection?

   _____

6. Name several things Christ does for the believer _____

   _____

V CONCERNING THE HOLY SPIRIT:

1. Is He a real person? _____

2. Do we receive the Holy Spirit when we believe? _____

   _____

3. Do you believe in being filled with the Spirit? _____

   _____

4. Is this the same as baptism of the Holy Spirit? _____

   _____

5. How may one be filled with the Spirit? _____
   Is one always filled with the Spirit from that time on? _____
   _____ Explain _____

6. Is speaking in tongues an evidence of being filled with the Holy Spirit?

   _____

   Do you speak in tongues? _____
   Have you ever spoken in tongues? _____
    Explain _____
   Do you believe this is a gift to be desired? _____

VI CONCERNING MAN:

1. Is man the product of evolution or of direct creation? _____

   _____

2. Is man born in sin? _____

3. Is man a sinner because of his environment? _____

   _____

4. Can the natural man do anything by himself to please God? __

   _____

5. Is a child a sinner before God when he is old enough to knowingly sin? _____

6. Are we all the children of God? _____ Explain _____

7. What is the one sin God cannot forgive? _____
8. Is everyone going to heaven? _____

VII CONCERNING SALVATION:

1. Explain how one can be saved. _____
_____
_____

2. What part do good works play in our salvation? _____
_____

3. What part does water baptism play in our salvation? _____
_____

4. Once a person is saved can he ever be lost? _____
5. What is sanctification? _____
6. Do you believe that when we are saved we have two natures? Explain _____

VIII CONCERNING THE CHRISTIAN LIFE:

1. Have you received Christ not only as your Savior but as the Lord and Manager of your life? _____
2. Do you lose your salvation when you sin? _____ Explain _____
_____

3. What do you lose when you sin? _____
4. What judgment goes on daily in your life? _____
5. What judgment is yet future for the Christian? _____
_____

6. What does God do when you sin? (use verses)
   a. take your name out of the Book of Life? _____
   b. not answer your prayers? _____
   c. paddle you? _____
   d. nothing? _____
   e. other? _____
7. Is temptation sin? _____ Why? _____
8. What should you do about all known sins? _____
_____

9. What does Christian separation mean to you? _____
_____

10. Tell what prayer can mean in your life _____
11. Do you believe it is important for a Christian to be baptized?

Explain: _____

12. Why is immersion more biblical than sprinkling? _____

_____

13. What important part should church membership play in the Christian's life? _____

_____

14. Can a Christian wife and mother become too busy "serving the Lord"? Explain _____

_____

IX CONCERNING FUTURE THINGS:

1. Do you believe in Heaven?_____Is it a literal place? _____
2. Do you believe in hell?_____ Does it continue forever?_____
3. Where will an unbeliever go when he dies? _____
4. Is there a second chance after death? _____
5. What is the rapture? _____
6. Do you believe in the premillennial *second coming* of Christ?

_____

7. Do you believe in a literal millennium? _____
8. Will the world get better and better until Jesus comes? _____

_____

9. What is the next great event to happen in God's marvelous plan? _____

_____

10. Name five rewards promised to Christians and what each will be given for.

    a. _____
    b. _____
    c. _____
    d. _____
    d. _____

X How long have you been a Christian? _____
Do you attend church regularly, and if so, where? _____

_____

EXAMPLE EVALUATION FORM

Women in the Bible study are asked to fill out an evaluation form at the end of each study year. This form from a recent year is typical. A tear-off section at the bottom of the last page helps locate helpers for the following year.

CHRIS-TOWN BIBLE STUDY EVALUATION SHEET

I. GENERAL INFORMATION
  1. Approximately how long have you been attending Chris-Town Bible Study? _____weeks _____months _____years
     How long have you been a Christian? _____
  2. Did you receive Jesus Christ as your own personal Savior while attending this Bible Study?_____ OR have you received assurance of salvation since coming to Chris-Town Bible Study? Approximately when? _____
  3. Were you able to be here: More than 50% _____ Less than 50% _____
  4. If you do not stay for the second hour small group studies, why?
     _____
     _____

II. CONCERNING THE FIRST HOUR STUDY IN I JOHN:
  1. What are the 3 main things we learned about God from I John? God is L_____ and L_____ and L_____.
  2. In what way has the study of I John changed your relationship to Jesus Christ? _____
     _____
  3. Which verse in I John has been outstanding to you? _____
     _____
  4. Give at least two reasons why you should love and believe in Jesus Christ: _____
     _____
  5. How can we recognize any false teachers? _____
     _____

6. From our study explain the difference between trying and trusting.
_____

7. How can you know for sure you are going to heaven? _____

8. Do you feel there is a good balance between the study of I John and the application to the home? _____
_____

   Why? _____
_____

9. What is your greatest area of need? _____
_____
_____

10. Name 3 things that you have learned in I John: _____
_____
_____
_____
_____

III. CONCERNING YOUR PRESENT SMALL GROUP STUDY
(We would like your honest opinion):
1. Was your group lecture or discussion? _____
2. Did the class move too fast or too slow? _____
3. Did the leader communicate the subject matter effectively?___
_____

   Explain _____
_____

4. Did you have assigned "homework"? _____ Did you do the work assigned? _____ If not, why? _____
_____

   Did you discuss your homework in class? _____
5. What new Bible truths have you learned? _____
_____
_____

6. Were you assigned verses to memorize each week? _____
   If so, were you faithful in doing the memory work? _____
   What have you learned in this group? _____
_____
_____

7. How has this group helped you in your everyday practical living?
   _____

8. What was the *main thing* you appreciated about your group?
   _____
   _____
   _____

9. How could the group as a whole have been more helpful to you?
   _____
   _____

10. Please make some constructive suggestions for improvement of your *small group* study:
    _____
    _____
    _____
    _____

11. Which type small group study do you prefer, lecture or discussion?
    _____

IV. OTHER INFORMATION:

1. If some friends you invited have not returned to Bible study, could you offer some reasons why? _____
   _____
   _____
   _____

— —

2. Check if you would like to help with one of these next fall:
   _____ Prayer Group (8:45 am)
   _____ Luncheon help
   _____ Coffee hostess (8:30 am)
   _____ Decorating
   _____ Phone calls
   _____ Lending or Tape library
   _____ Guest table
   If you checked to help in any of above areas, please give your
   NAME _____
   PHONE _____

DIVORCE IS NEVER NECESSARY

by Paul D. Meier, M.D.

It took 12 years of college, graduate school, medical school and psychiatry residency for me to become a full-fledged psychiatrist. Many people assume that, after all that training, I should be magically able to "cure" any kind of emotional problem or mental illness in three or four 45-minute sessions — even if my patient has been forming those maladaptive patterns for 20 or 30 years. And since I am a committed evangelical Christian who not only believes in the inerrancy of Scripture but uses scriptural principles extensively in my practice, my Christian patients tend to expect "overnight cures" even more than the non-Christians.

Last year a 29-year-old young lady came to see me at my office and spent our first 45-minute session talking about her husband. He had been reared in a home where there was a weak, passive father and a domineering, overprotective mother (which is the case in about 85% of all mental illnesses). His mother had spoiled him all his life, giving him everything he wanted. She had also done most of his thinking for him, so that he had developed a very passive-dependent personality. He had been married previously and was now working on his second marriage. He was drinking quite a bit, smoking pot with great regularity, and skipping work (calling in "sick") at least one day a week. He was spending nearly all of his free time "with the boys," almost totally ignoring his wife.

His wife sat in my office, telling me that unless I could dramatically change him within the next few weeks she was going to divorce him. I was supposed to accomplish this in spite of the fact that he had refused to come in with her for sessions.

As a Christian counselor, what do you do at this point? Do you throw your hands up in the air and say, "Impossible!"? Do you tell her to keep suffering and send her on her way? Do you tell her to go ahead and use the "Great American Cop-out" and to be more careful the next time she picks a husband? Many secular counselors and too many so-called "Christian" counselors choose the latter route since it appears to be the easy way out, and usually that's what the counselee wants to hear anyway!

In reality, there are only three choices for any person who is involved in an unhappy marriage: (1) divorce — the greatest copout and by far the most immature choice; (2) tough out the marriage without working to improve it — another immature decision but not quite as irresponsible as divorce, and (3) maturely face up to personal hangups and choose to build an intimate marriage out of the existing one — the only really mature choice to make.

I have depicted a very gloomy picture of what to expect in a marriage counseling situation. Before you give up totally on marriage counseling, I would like to present some more optimistic facts and guiding principles:

1. MARTIAL CONFLICT PATIENTS ARE THE EASIEST TO HELP

a. Out of all the vast array of psychiatric patients that I see (ranging from childhood schizophrenics to senile patients with organic brain syndromes), marital conflict patients are the easiest to help and most rewarding to work with.

b. I have seen scores of marital conflict cases similar to the one described above, including many where adultery was an additional factor. In all the cases where both marriage partners agreed to come in for at least four sessions together (even if they had already filed for divorce), not a single couple has ended up getting a divorce.

c. Not only have these couples chosen not to divorce, but in every case — once they got over the hurdle of deciding to make the best of their present marriage — significant improvements have been made in their marital and other interpersonal relationships.

d. There is no such thing as a perfect marriage. Whenever a married couple declares they have been married for 20 to 30 years without an argument, I tell them "Well, then, one of you isn't necessary!"

2. THERE IS NO SUCH THING AS "INCOMPATIBLE PERSONALITIES"

I get tired of hearing people say that so-and-so "had to" get a divorce because they found out that they had "incompatible personalities." As a trained Christian psychiatrist, I can honestly and emphatically say that this excuse is no more than a cop-out used by couples who are too proud and lazy to work out their own hangups. Instead of facing them, they run away by divorcing and remarrying. Then there are four miserable people instead of just two.

Why spread misery? Bad marriages are contagious! Numerous psychiatric research studies have shown that when couples with neurotic marriage relationships get divorced — no matter how good their intentions may be — they nearly always remarry into the very same type of neurotic relationship they had before.

3. DIVORCE IS NEVER NECESSARY

According to the best research surveys which I have studied, it is estimated that, in over 50% of American marriages, either one or both marriage partners have committed adultery some time during the marriage. In a great many cases, the adultery was a one-time experience, committed at a weak moment, and in the long run, did not significantly alter the marriage relationship.

A number of patients have confessed to me in a therapy session that they have had a brief sexual encounter with someone other than their mate. Many of them have carried around tremendous guilt for months or even years. They ask if they should tell their husbands or wives about it. I generally share 1 John 1:9 with them, urge them to confess to God the sin of adultery just as they would any other sin, encourage them to forgive themselves since God forgives them, and advocate they *not* ever bring up this particular sin with their mates.

Some patients have insisted on revealing it to their mates, supposedly to get it off their chests, when in reality in my opinion, their unconscious motivation was to tell their mates in order to express pent-up anger toward them. That even may have been the motivation behind having the affair in the first place.

The wounds from adultery can run very deep, but I have been amazed by the tremendous capacity within mature human beings to forgive one another. Patients have told me that they never thought they would be able to forgive their mate if he (or she) ever committed adultery — until it actually happened. Then they were amazed at their own ability to forgive. They realized how much they wanted to restore intimate fellowship with their mate.

I never recommended divorce even in cases of adultery. There are, of course, situations in which one partner has actually left home for an extended period of time to "shack up" with someone in an adulterous relationship, refuses to return home, and rejects counseling. I still would *not* recommend divorce, because Christ instructed us in Matthew 19:6, "What therefore God hath joined together, let not man put asunder."

In the end, it must be a decision made by the counselee. I point out what Scripture has to say about it, including the fact that Christ *permits* (not commands) divorce in Matthew 19:9 — but only in cases where the mate has committed "fornication." The Greek word translated as "fornication" is *porneia* (pronounced "por-nayah"), which means specifically to have sexual intercourse with a person of the opposite sex other than one's mate. I have personally consulted with several evangelical theologians from conservative seminaries who interpret the original Greek records of Christ's comments on divorce to imply that divorce and remarriage are permissible — but only in cases where the other marriage partner has committed adultery.

4. LOVE THAT IS LOST CAN BE REFOUND

Many reasonable people who divorce their mates use the ridiculous excuse, "I divorced my husband because I didn't love him any more." I generally reply, "So what?" Love is important, but it is only a feeling, and it is a feeling that rises and falls like the ocean's tide.

Our feelings, including the feeling of love, are determined by our *actions*, and not the other way around. If you act like you love someone, the feeling will inevitably follow.

The 29-year-old young lady that I mentioned at the beginning of this article had her mind pretty much made up that she should divorce her husband because she didn't love him any more. I asked her if she would be willing to act like she loved him for a couple of weeks to see if the feeling would follow. She agreed to try it. She even came up with some good ideas about how she would go about it.

In individual sessions we dealt with some of her own hangups. I was not surprised to find out that she was very similar in personality to the domineering mother who reared her husband. She personally thought of ways to turn the leadership in the home back over to her husband. She acted like she trusted him to handle the finances (even though she really didn't).

To her amazement, within a week she started to regain her love for her husband. He responded to her changed attitude toward him by actually becoming more responsible. He even requested to come with her to her therapy sessions.

I saw them together (which is the only good way to do marriage counseling) once a week from then on for a period of several months. After several sessions of open, three-way discussion, the husband became bitterly aware of the fact that he was an overgrown, spoiled child who was married to a substitute mother — and he wept. But from that awareness came genuine growth, as he assumed adult responsibilities for the first time and as his wife relinquished her mothering instincts toward him.

Both of them learned to get in touch with angry feelings and to talk them out with each other rather than to allow their anger to accumulate inside until they acted it out immaturely. I taught them this from Ephesians 4:26: "Be ye angry, and sin not; let not the sun go down upon your wrath." *Married* couples should never go to bed at night with angry feelings still pent up inside. When my own wife and children become angry at me for some reason, they tell me so, and we sit down and talk it out calmly and openly. It promotes real trust and unity.

I can't take the credit for inventing the technique of restoring love by acting like you love someone. It's a technique that God Himself used in Revelation 2:4-5. In this passage of Scripture Christ compliments the local church at Ephesus for several things, but then tells them, "I have somewhat against thee, because thou hast left thy first love" (verse 4).

Christ then shares with them three steps that will enable them to rediscover the original love for Him that they lost. 1. "*Remember* therefore from whence thou art fallen." Christ wanted them to remember what it was like when they were intimately in love with Him. 2. "*Repent*." The Lord was asking them to *choose* to love Him intimately again. 3. "*Do the first works*." Christ was suggesting they do the things they had done when they were intimately in love with Him before. He knew that the feeling of love would follow if they would only act like they did when they loved Him earlier. I am continually amazed by the vast number of couples who have been married from 5 to 50 years without ever learning how to communicate their feelings to each other on a gut level. Sometimes they can communicate how they feel about their mate to a third party, such as a friend, pastor or psychiatrist, but they have tremendous difficulty communicating their feelings to each other face to face.

5. SLIGHT IMPROVEMENT IN COMMUNICATIONAL ABILITY SIGNIFICANTLY IMPROVES THE OVERALL MARRIAGE RELATIONSHIP.

When a husband and wife come to my office for conjoint therapy, they consistently tell me (rather than their mate) how they feel about each other. At this point I ask the communicating mate to turn to the other and express the feeling directly.

I remember a number of occasions when the 29-year-old young lady I have told you about would become angry about something her husband would say. In the early sessions, she would just "look" angry. In later sessions she learned to tell me, "Dr. Meier, I really feel angry about what my husband just said." But then, toward the end of our sessions together, she was able to turn directly to her husband and say, "Honey, I'm feeling angry toward you right now for that cutting remark. Can we talk about it?"

Many of the couples I have counseled have told me that the 45 minutes in my office is the only 45 minutes during the week that they are able to communicate honestly with each other. But the longer they are in therapy, the more they learn to communicate intimately and honestly at home.

In the first few sessions of marriage counseling I am usually quite confrontational and directive, but the longer a couple is in therapy, the more I can just sit back and observe them doing therapy on each other. I only need to add occasional interjections to bring something to their awareness that they have missed.

Some couples who have been sexually impotent for months regain their sexual function after six months or so of this type of communicational therapy — even if the subject of sex seldom comes up. As a psychiatrist, I believe the sexual function is a symptom of a couple's verbal communication ability, emotional intimacy and spiritual closeness. Many times an improved spiritual relationship with God also seems to improve a couple's sexual intimacy.

I personally believe that lack of self-worth (inferiority feelings) is probably the number one factor that limits our ability to love our mates more intimately. Christ told us that the greatest commandment is to love God with all our heart, soul, mind and strength: and to love our neighbors as ourselves (Mark 12:30-31). The Apostle Paul taught us, "He that loveth his wife loveth himself" (Ephesians 5:28).

6. SELF-ACCEPTANCE LEADS TO MATE ACCEPTANCE.

People who don't love and accept themselves in a healthy way compensate for their feelings of inferiority by acting out of false pride, which is a serious sin (Proverbs 6:17). Solomon taught us that "only by pride cometh contention" (Proverbs 13:10). Marital conflicts are not only evidence of psychological hang-ups, but of a sin problem — the sin of false pride.

Psychiatrists know that when people refuse to face up to, accept, and deal with their own hangups, they unconsciously lie to themselves by rejecting other people who have similar hangups. This defense mechanism is known as projection. If I do not accept myself, I will find it extremely difficult to intimately accept my wife, since she has a few behavior traits that are similar to my own. Christ told us to quit projecting in Matthew 7:3-5, where he stated, "And why beholdest thou the mote that is in thy brother's eye, but considerest not the beam that is in thine own eye? Or how wilt thou say to thy brother, let me pull out the mote out of thine eye; and a beam is in thine own eye? Thou hypocrite, first cast out the beam out of thine own eye; and then thou shalt see clearly to cast out the mote out of thy brother's eye."

7. MARRIAGE GROUP COUNSELING IS EFFECTIVE AND EFFICIENT IN THE LOCAL CHURCH.

For churches who would like to institute marriage group counseling, I recommend a good book that gives details: *The Pastor and Marriage Group Counseling*. by Reverand Richard Wilke. I am extremely excited by the rapid growth of "body life" concepts and practices in local evangelical churches across America. In order to meet the tremendous needs of God's people today, the local church must be biblical (sound in Bible doctrine and teaching), soul-winning (introducing others to a saving knowledge of Jesus Christ) and relational (meeting needs for intimate relationships with each other). A solid church needs all three of these legs to stand on.

The "relational" leg has been the most neglected among many Bible-believing churches in both America and Europe in recent decades. In Hebrews 10:24-25, we are instructed, "And let us consider one another to provoke unto love and to good works: not forsaking the assembling of ourselves together, as the manner of some is; but exhorting one another: and so much the more, as ye see the day approaching." Various types of gatherings ranging from Bible study to marriage enrichment groups are springing up in evangelical churches to meet this real need — especially as the day of Christ's return appears imminent.

8. SUCCESSFUL MARRIAGE COUNSELING TAKES FAITH.

Marriage counseling is one of the most rewarding ways a person — whether a professional counselor or not — can serve both God and our fellowman. But successful marriage counseling takes *faith*. Faith that God can heal any wound. Faith that people can learn to accept themselves. Faith that people can put away childish games and learn to relate intimately.

The 29-year-old young lady I described in this article seemed to be in an impossible situation and headed for divorce when I saw her for the first time in my office a year ago, but faith in her and her husband resulted in works. It has been six months since I have seen this couple. I received a letter from them a few weeks ago thanking me for helping them build an intimate marriage out of apparent disaster.

Building a healthy marriage with preventative "medicine" and a growing Christ-centered faith is never "easy." But when a couple is motivated to have faith that God can and will heal their marriage, followed by their own hard work, divorce is *never* necessary.

Reprinted with permission of the author and publisher from **United Evangelical Action** *(Fall 1975), official publication of the National Association of Evangelicals.*